RENAL DIET COOKBOOK

101 EASY-TO-MAKE RECIPES LOW IN SODIUM, PROTEIN, POTASSIUM AND PHOSPHORUS FOR YOUR KIDNEY DISEASE

ISBN-13:9781543006551

ISBN-10: 1543006558

Contents

Chapter 2: Lunch Recipes

Chapter 3: DINNER Recipes 100

CHAPTER 1: BREAKFAST RECIPES

POWER-BOOSTING SMOOTHIE (2 SERVINGS, SERVING: 1 GLASS)

Per Serving, Calories: 242 - Fat: 7g - Carbs: 23.8g - Protein: 23.2g - Fiber: 2.6g - Potassium: 263mg - Sodium: 63mg

Ingredients:

- 1½ cups of frozen blueberries

- ½ cup of non-dairy whipped topping

- 2 scoops of whey protein powder

- ½ cup of water

Directions:

1. In a high speed blender, add all ingredients and pulse till smooth.

2. Transfer into 2 serving glass and serve immediately.

DISTINCTIVE PINEAPPLE SMOOTHIE (2 SERVINGS, SERVING: 1 GLASS)

Per Serving, Calories: 117 - Fat: 2.1g - Carbs: 18.2g - Protein: 22.7g - Fiber: 1.7g - Potassium: 296mg - Sodium: 81mg

Ingredients:

- 1½ cups of pineapple

- 2 scoops of vanilla whey protein powder

- 1 cup of water

- ¼ cup of crushed ice cubes

Directions:

1. In a high speed blender, add all ingredients and pulse till smooth.

2. Transfer into 2 serving glass and serve immediately.

STRENGTHENING SMOOTHIE BOWL (2 SERVINGS, SERVING: 1 BOWL)

Per Serving, Calories: 176- Fat: 2.1g - Carbs: 27g - Protein: 15.1g - Fiber: 4.1g - Potassium: 242mg - Sodium: 72mg

Ingredients:

- 2 cups of frozen blueberries

- 1/3 cup of unsweetened almond milk

- ¼ cup of fat-free plain Greek yogurt

- 2 tbsp. of whey protein powder

- ¼ cup of fresh blueberries

Directions:

1. In a blender, add blueberries and pulse for about 1 minute.

2. Add almond milk, yogurt and protein powder and pulse till desired consistency.

3. Transfer the mixture into 2 bowls evenly.

4. Serve with the topping of fresh blueberries.

Nutritive Breakfast Bowl (5 servings, serving: 1 bowl)

Per Serving, Calories: 91- Fat: 3g - Carbs: 15.7g - Protein: 1g - Fiber: 1.6g - Potassium: 93mg - Sodium: 5mg

Ingredients:

- 1½ cups of water plus extra if needed

- ½ cups of uncooked wheat berries

- 1 tbsp. of canola oil

- 1 cored and thinly sliced medium pear

- ½ cup of fresh cranberries

- 1 tsp. of finely grated fresh ginger

- 2 tbsp. of maple syrup

- 1 tsp. of finely grated fresh lemon zest

- ½ tsp. of ground cinnamon

Directions:

1. In a pan, add water and wheat berries and bring to a boil on medium-high heat,

2. Reduce the heat to low and simmer, covered for about 30 minutes.

3. Add extra water if needed and simmer for about 15-20 minutes r till desired doneness.

4. Meanwhile in a skillet, heat oil on medium heat.

5. Add pear slices and cook for about 3-4 minutes.

6. Add cranberries and ginger and cook for about 2-3 minutes.

7. Stir in cooked wheat berries, maple syrup, lemon zest and cinnamon and cook for about 1-2 minutes.

8. Serve warm.

FALL-TIME APPLE OMELET (2 SERVINGS, SERVING: 1 PORTION)

Per Serving, Calories: 244- Fat: 16.3g - Carbs: 14.4g - Protein: 11.7g - Fiber: 1.8g - Potassium: 262mg - Sodium: 152mg

Ingredients:

- 3 eggs

- ¼ cup of 1% low-fat milk

- 1 tbsp. of water

- Freshly ground black pepper, to taste

- 1 tbsp. of olive oil

- 1 peeled, cored and thinly sliced large apple

- ¾ cup of thinly sliced sweet onion

- 2 tbsp. of shredded low-fat cheddar cheese

Directions:

1. Preheat the oven to 400 degrees F.

2. In a bowl, add eggs, milk, water and black pepper and beat well.

3. In a small ovenproof skillet, heat oil on medium heat.

4. Add apple and onion and sauté for about 5-6 minutes.

5. With the spatula, spread the apple mixture in the bottom of the skillet.

6. Sprinkle with the cheddar cheese and top with egg mixture evenly.

7. Transfer the skillet into the oven and bake for about 10-12 minutes.

8. Remove from the oven and cut into 2 equal portions.

9. Serve warm.

AWESOME CLAM OMELET (4 SERVINGS, SERVING: 1 PORTION)

Per Serving, Calories: 162- Fat: 13.2g - Carbs: 3.4g - Protein: 8g - Fiber: 0g -
Potassium: 98mg - Sodium: 142mg

Ingredients:

- 5 large eggs

- 1/8 tsp. of freshly ground black pepper

- ¼ cup of shelled clams

- 2 tsp. of cornstarch

- 2 tbsp. of olive oil

Directions:

1. In a bowl, add eggs and black pepper and beat well.

2. Stir in clans and cornstarch.

3. In a frying pan, heat oil on low heat.

4. Add the egg mixture and cook for about 2 minutes.

5. Carefully, tilt the pan and cook for about 2 minutes more or till desired doneness.

6. Transfer the omelet into a plate and cut into 4 wedges.

FOOLPROOF VEGGIE OMELET (3 SERVINGS, SERVING: 1 PORTION)

Per Serving, Calories: 157- Fat: 10.8g - Carbs: 8.2g - Protein: 8.3g - Fiber: 1.3g - Potassium: 287mg - Sodium: 81mg

Ingredients:

- 2 large eggs

- 2 large egg whites

- ¼ cup of 1% low-fat milk

- 1/8 tsp. of ground cumin

- 1/8 tsp. of freshly ground black pepper

- 1½ tbsp. of olive oil

- 1 tsp. of minced garlic

- 2 tbsp. of chopped scallion

- 2 tbsp. of seeded and chopped red bell pepper

- 2 tbsp. of chopped fresh mushrooms

Directions:

1. In a bowl, add eggs, egg whites, milk, cumin and black pepper and beat well. Keep aside.

2. In a skillet, heat oil on medium heat.

3. Add garlic and sauté for about 30 seconds.

4. Add scallion, bell peppers and mushroom and cook for about 4-5 minutes.

5. Place the egg mixture over the vegetables evenly.

6. Reduce the heat to medium-low and cook, covered for about 1-2 minutes.

7. Uncover and carefully, tilt the pan and cook for about 2 minutes more.

8. Transfer the omelet into a plate and cut into 2 wedges.

FLUFFY SCRAMBLED EGGS (2 SERVINGS, SERVING: 1 PORTION)

Per Serving, Calories: 144- Fat: 10g - Carbs: 1.4g - Protein: 12.3g - Fiber: 0g - Potassium: 153mg - Sodium: 137mg

Ingredients:

- 4 beaten eggs

- 2 tsp. of dried dill weed

- Freshly ground black pepper, to taste

- 1 tbsp. of crumbled goat cheese

Directions:

1. Heat a nonstick skillet on medium heat.

2. Add the beaten eggs and sprinkle with dill weed and black pepper.

3. Cook for about 2-3 minutes, stirring continuously.

4. Sprinkle with goat cheese and serve hot.

GREAT EGGS & VEGGIE SCRAMBLE (2 SERVINGS, SERVING: 1 PORTION)

Per Serving, Calories: 243- Fat: 12.7g - Carbs: 21.8g - Protein: 12.1g - Fiber: 3.5g - Potassium: 289mg - Sodium: 118mg

Ingredients:

- ½ of (6-ounce) corn tortilla
- 2 eggs
- 2 egg whites
- 1 tbsp. olive oil
- 3 chopped scallions
- 2 (¼-inch thick) tomato slices

Directions:

1. In a microwave safe plate, pace the tortilla and microwave for about 1½-2 minutes.

2. Remove from the microwave and crush the tortilla into chops size pieces.

3. In a bowl, add egg and egg whites and beat well.

4. Heat a nonstick skillet on medium heat.

5. Add egg mixture and cook for about 2 minutes, stirring continuously.

6. With a slotted spoon transfer the scrambled eggs into a bowl.

7. In the same skillet, heat oil on medium heat.

8. Add scallion and sauté for about 1 minute.

9. Add tomato slices, crushed tortilla and scrambled eggs and cook for about 1-2 minutes or till desired doneness.

WONDERFUL MICROWAVE SCRAMBLE (2 SERVINGS, SERVING: 1 PORTION)

Per Serving, Calories: 112- Fat: 4.8g - Carbs: 2.7g - Protein: 14g - Fiber: 0g - Potassium: 241mg - Sodium: 142mg

Ingredients:

- ¼ cup of 1% low-fat milk

- 2 eggs

- 4 egg whites

- ¼ cup finely chopped fresh mushrooms

- Freshly ground black pepper, to taste

Directions:

1. Grease 2 (12-ounce) coffee mugs.

2. In a bowl, add milk, eggs and egg whites and beat till well combined.

3. Stir in onion.

4. Divide the egg mixture into greased mugs evenly and microwave for about 45 seconds.

5. Remove from the mugs from microwave and stir well.

6. Microwave for about 30-45 seconds more.

AMAZING APPLE STRATA (12 SERVINGS, SERVING: 1 PORTION)

Per Serving, Calories: 343- Fat: 12.7g - Carbs: 29.6g - Protein: 9.6g - Fiber: 1.3g - Potassium: 144mg - Sodium: 350mg

Ingredients:

- 1¼ cups of unsweetened almond milk

- 1¼ cups of half-and-half creamer

- 1/3 cup of melted unsalted margarine

- ¼ cup of pancake syrup

- 8 large eggs

- 1 pound of cubed cinnamon bread loaf

- 8-ounce of cubed low-fat cream cheese

- 1 cup of peeled, cored and chopped apple

- 1 tsp. of ground cinnamon

Directions:

1. Grease a 13x9-inch baking dish.

2. In a bowl, add milk, half-and-half creamer, margarine, pancake syrup and eggs and beat till well combined. Keep aside.

3. In the bottom of prepared baking dish, place half of bread cubes evenly, followed by cream cheese and apple.

4. Sprinkle with cinnamon and top with remaining bread cubes evenly.

5. Pour egg mixture on top evenly.

6. With aplastic rap, cover the baking dish and refrigerate for overnight.

7. Preheat the oven to 325 degrees F.

8. Bake, uncovered for about 50 minutes.

9. Remove from the oven and keep aside for about 10 minutes before serving.

10. Cut into 12 equal sized pieces and serve.

DELISH VEGGIE STRATA (12 SERVINGS, SERVING: 1 PORTION)

Per Serving, Calories: 149- Fat: 5.8g - Carbs: 15g - Protein: 8.9g - Fiber: 1.2g - Potassium: 87mg - Sodium: 191mg

Ingredients:

- 2 cups of unsweetened rice milk

- 12 eggs

- 1 cup of finely shredded part-skim mozzarella cheese

- ½ cup of seeded and chopped red bell pepper

- ½ cup of chopped fresh mushrooms

- ½ cup of chopped onion

- 2 tsp. of minced garlic

- 1 tsp. of crushed dried oregano

- 1 tsp. of crushed dried basil

- 6 crumbled English muffin toasting bread slices

- Freshly ground black pepper, to taste

Directions:

1. Grease a 13x9-inch baking dish.

2. In a bowl, add rice milk and eggs and beat till well combined.

3. Add remaining ingredients except crumbled bread and stir to combine well.

4. In the bottom of prepared baking dish, place the crumbled bread evenly.

5. Pour egg mixture on top evenly.

6. With aplastic rap, cover the baking dish and refrigerate for about 8-10 hours.

7. Preheat the oven to 350 degrees F.

8. Bake, uncovered for about 1 hour.

9. Remove from the oven and keep aside for about 10 minutes before serving.

10. Cut into 12 equal sized pieces and serve.

WEEKEND MORNING FRITTATA (5 SERVINGS, SERVING: 1 PORTION)

Per Serving, Calories: 88- Fat: 5g - Carbs: 4.7g - Protein: 6.4g - Fiber: 1.1g - Potassium: 261mg - Sodium: 116mg

Ingredients:

- 2 large eggs

- 4 egg whites

- 1/8 tsp. of ground cumin

- 1/8 tsp. of ground turmeric

- Pinch of salt

- Freshly ground black pepper, to taste

- 1 tbsp. of canola oil

- 3 minced garlic cloves

- 2 tbsp. of chopped green chili

- ½ cup of chopped onion

- 2 cups of thinly sliced zucchini

- 1 chopped small tomato

- 2 tsp. of chopped fresh parsley

Directions:

1. In a bowl, add eggs, egg whites and spices and beat till well combined. Keep aside.

2. In a 12-inch nonstick skillet, heat oil on medium heat.

3. Add onion and sauté for about 2 minutes.

4. Add garlic and green chili and sauté for about 1 minute.

5. Add zucchini and sauté for about 2-3 minutes.
6. Sprinkle with tomato and parsley and immediately, top with egg mixture evenly.

7. Reduce the heat to low and cook, covered for about 10 minutes.

8. Remove from the heat and cut into 5 equal sized portions and serve.

YUMMY FRITTATA (7 SERVINGS, SERVING: 1 PORTION)

Per Serving, Calories: 223- Fat: 5.7g - Carbs: 28.5g - Protein: 13.3g - Fiber: 0g
- Potassium: 282mg - Sodium: 148mg

Ingredients:

- 4 large eggs

- 2 large egg whites

- 2½ cups of fat-free milk

- Freshly ground black pepper, to taste

- 2 tsp. of olive oil

- 2½ cups of cooked spaghetti

- 2-ounce of finely shredded low-fat mozzarella cheese

- 1/3 cup of chopped scallion

- 2 tbsp. of chopped fresh basil leaves

Directions:

1. In a bowl, add eggs, egg whites and black pepper and beat till well combined. Keep aside.

2. In a medium nonstick skillet, heat oil on medium heat.

3. In the bottom of the skillet, place the spaghetti evenly and cook for about 2 minutes.

4. Top with egg mixture evenly and sprinkle with cheese, scallion and basil.

5. Cook, covered for about 8 minutes.

6. Remove from the heat and cut into 5 equal sized portions and serve.

KID'S FAVORITE EGG ON TOAST (2 SERVINGS, SERVING: 1 SLICE WITH 1 EGG)

Per Serving, Calories: 104- Fat: 5.8g - Carbs: 5.1g - Protein: 7.8g - Fiber: 0g - Potassium: 77mg - Sodium: 155mg

Ingredients:

- 2 white bread slices

- 2 large eggs

- Olive oil cooking spray, as required

- Freshly ground black pepper, to taste

- 2 tsp. of low-fat grated Parmesan cheese

Directions:

1. With a biscuit cutter, press a hole in the center of each bread slice.

2. Grease a nonstick skillet with cooking spray and heat on medium-low heat.

3. Arrange a bread slice in the skillet and carefully, crack the egg in the center of the hole.

4. Cook for about 30-45 seconds.

5. Sprinkle with black pepper and carefully, flip the slice.

6. Cook for about 1 minute or till desired doneness of egg yolk.

7. Repeat with remaining slice and egg.

8. Sprinkle with parmesan and serve.

CREATIVE BREAKFAST PARCELS (4 SERVINGS, SERVING: 1 PARCEL)

Per Serving, Calories: 350- Fat: 9.2g - Carbs: 52.4g - Protein: 10.3g - Fiber: 2g - Potassium: 188mg - Sodium: 137mg

Ingredients:

- 1 cup of warm water

- 1¼ tsp. of dry yeast

- 2 cups of all-purpose white flour

- 1 tbsp. of sugar

- 1 tsp. of garlic powder

- 1 tbsp. of olive oil

- ¾ cup of low-cholesterol liquid egg substitute

- ¼ cup of softened low-fat cream cheese

Directions:

1. In a large bowl, add warm water.

2. Add yeast and stir till dissolve completely.

3. Add flour, sugar, garlic powder and oil and mix till a soft dough forms.

4. Transfer the dough into a greased bowl.

5. With a plastic wrap, cover the bowl and keep aside for about 5 minutes.

6. Preheat the oven to 350 degrees F.

7. Place the dough onto a lightly floured surface and roll into1/2-inch thickness.

8. Cut the dough into 4 equal sized pieces and serve.

9. Heat a nonstick frying pan on medium heat. Lightly, grease a baking sheet.

10. Add egg substitute and cook for about 2 minutes, stirring continuously.

11. Stir in cream cheese and remove from heat.

12. Divide egg mixture over each dough piece evenly.

13. Fold the dough over egg mixture by pinching the edges.

14. Cut the top of parcel to remove the steam.

15. Spray each parcel with a little cooking spray.

16. Arrange the parcels onto the prepared baking sheet in a single layer.

17. Bake for about 15-20minutes.

BEST-EVER BLUEBERRY MUFFINS (12 SERVINGS, SERVING: 1 MUFFIN)

Per Serving, Calories: 165- Fat: 5.4g - Carbs: 27.3g - Protein: 2.8g - Fiber: 1.4g - Potassium: 124mg - Sodium: 18mg

Ingredients:

- 2 cups of all-purpose white flour

- ½ cup of granulated sugar

- 2 tsp. of baking powder

- 1 cup of unsweetened brown rice milk

- 1 lightly beaten large eggs

- ¼ cup of vegetable oil

- 1 cup of frozen blueberries

- 1 tbsp. of finely grated fresh lemon zest

Directions:

1. Preheat the oven to 375 degrees F. Lightly, grease a 12 cups of a muffin pan.

2. In a bowl, mix together flour, sugar and baking powder.

3. In another bowl, add rice milk, eggs and oil and beat till well combined.

4. Add egg mixture into flour mixture and mix till just moistened.

5. Gently, fold in blueberries and lemon zest.

6. Transfer the mixture into prepared muffin cups evenly.

7. Bake for about 25 manures or till a toothpick inserted in the center comes out clean.

DELISH SAVORY MUFFINS (12 SERVINGS, SERVING: 1 MUFFIN)

Per Serving, Calories: 83- Fat: 5.2g - Carbs: 1g - Protein: 8.1g - Fiber: 0g - Potassium: 95mg - Sodium: 74mg

Ingredients:

- ½ cup of unsalted cooked and shredded chicken

- 1/3 cup of seeded and chopped green bell pepper

- 1/3 cup of chopped fresh mushrooms

- 1/3 cup of chopped onion

- 12 large eggs

- Freshly ground black pepper, to taste

Directions:

1. Preheat the oven to 350 degrees F. Line a 12 cups muffin pan with paper liner.

2. In a bowl, mix together the chicken and vegetables.

3. In another bowl, add eggs and black pepper and beat well.

4. Divide the bacon mixture into the prepared muffin cups about 2/3 full.

5. Pour egg mixture over the chicken mixture, leaving about ¼-inch space from the top.

6. Bake for about 25 minutes.

7. Remove the muffin pan from the oven and place onto a wire rack to for about 10 minutes. Carefully, invert the muffins onto wire rack and serve warm.

WHOLESOME BREAD (10 SERVINGS, SERVING: 1 SLICE)

Per Serving, Calories: 209- Fat: 8.5g - Carbs: 29.2g - Protein: 3.4g - Fiber: 0.9g - Potassium: 124mg -Sodium: 49mg

Ingredients:

- 1 2/3 cups of all-purpose white flour

- ¾ tsp. of baking powder

- ¼ tsp. of baking soda

- ½ tsp. of ground cinnamon

- ¼ cup of olive oil

- ½ cup of granulated sugar

- 1/3 cup of applesauce

- 2 egg whites

- 1 cup of peeled, cored and chopped Granny Smith apple

- 2/3 cup of low-fat sour cream

Directions:

1. Preheat the oven to 350 degrees F. Lightly, grease an 8½-4¾-inch loaf pan.

2. In a bowl, mix together flour, baking powder, baking soda and cinnamon.

3. In another bowl, add oil and sugar and beat till well combined.

4. Add applesauce and egg whites and beat till well combined.

5. Add egg mixture into flour mixture and mix till just moistened.

6. Gently, fold in apple and sour cream.

7. Transfer the mixture into prepared loaf pan evenly.

8. Bake for about 50-55 manures or till a toothpick inserted in the center comes out clean.
9. Remove the loaf pan from the oven and place onto a wire rack to for about 10 minutes.

10. Carefully, invert the bread onto wire rack to cool completely.

11. With a sharp knife, cut into 10 equal sized slices and serve.

QUICKEST FRENCH TOASTS (4 SERVINGS, SERVING: 1 FRENCH TOAST)

Per Serving, Calories: 165- Fat: 12.8g - Carbs: 7 g - Protein: 6.5g - Fiber: 0.5g - Potassium: 164mg - Sodium: 190mg

Ingredients:

- 1¼ cups of unsweetened almond milk

- 4 eggs

- 4 (¾-inch thick) trimmed and diagonally sliced white bread slices

- 2 tbsp. of olive oil

- 3 tbsp. of sugar-free syrup

Directions:

1. Preheat the oven to 400 degrees F. Arrange a baking sheet in the oven to heat.

2. In a bowl, add almond milk and eggs and beat slightly.

3. Dip each bread slice in egg mixture evenly.

4. In a skillet, heat oil on medium heat.

5. Add bread slices and cook for about 1 minute per side.

6. Now, arrange the slices onto hot baking sheet in a single layer.

7. Bake for about 4 minutes.

8. Drizzle with syrup and serve.

EASIEST FRENCH TOAST CASSEROLE (2 SERVINGS, SERVING: 1 PORTION)

Per Serving, Calories: 128- Fat: 4.3g - Carbs: 7.4g - Protein: 14g - Fiber: 0g - Potassium: 208mg - Sodium: 226mg

Ingredients:

- 2 cubed white bread slices

- 2 tsp. of softened unsalted butter

- 1 cup of slightly beaten egg whites

- 2 tbsp. of sugar-free syrup

Directions:

1. In a microwave safe bowl, add the cubed bread and top with egg whites evenly.

2. Drizzle with syrup and microwave for about 1 minute.

3. Remove from microwave and with a spoon, push away the edges of egg whites.

4. Microwave for about 1 minute more.

5. Remove from microwave and divide into 2 portions. Serve warm.

FUSS-FREE BAGEL SANDWICH (2 SERVINGS, SERVING: ½ BAGEL)

Per Serving, Calories: 120- Fat: 4g - Carbs: 17.4g - Protein: 4.1g - Fiber: 1.4g - Potassium: 131mg - Sodium: 159mg

Ingredients:

- 1 (2-ounce) bagels, sliced

- 2 tbsp. of low-fat cream cheese

- 4 red onion slices

- 4 (¼-inch thick) tomato slices

Directions:

1. Heat a nonstick skillet on medium heat.

2. Add bagel slices and toast for about 30 seconds per side.

3. Spread cream cheese over each bagel slice evenly.

4. Place onion and tomato slices over 2 bagel slices, cut side down.

5. Cover with remaining slices.

6. Cut the sandwich in half and serve.

Iconic French Toast Casserole (8 servings, serving: 1 portion)

Per Serving, Calories: 276- Fat: 7.4g - Carbs: 41.1g - Protein: 10.8g - Fiber: 1g - Potassium: 101mg -Sodium: 119mg

Ingredients:

- 1 pound of day-old French bread loaf

- 6 tbsp. of softened low-fat cream cheese

- 6 tbsp. of strawberry jelly

- 1 cup of fat-free milk

- 6 eggs

- 1 tsp. of vanilla extract

Directions:

1. Cut the bread loaf 1nto 6 equal sized slices.

2. Spread cream cheese over 8 slices evenly, followed by the jelly evenly.

3. Top with remaining bread slice to make sandwiches.

4. In a bowl, add milk, eggs and vanilla extract and beat till well combined.

5. Grease a 13x9-inch baking dish.

6. Arrange the sandwiches into the prepared baking dish in a single layer and top with egg mixture evenly.

7. Cover the baking dish and refrigerate for overnight.

8. Preheat the oven to 350 degrees F.

9. With a piece of the foil, cover the baking dish and bake for about 55 minutes.

10. Remove the foil and bake for about 5 minutes more.

FRENCH STYLE CREPES (15 SERVINGS, SERVING: 1 CREPE)

Per Serving, Calories: 72- Fat: 3.4g - Carbs: 7.4g - Protein: 2.8g - Fiber: 0.6g - Potassium: 84mg - Sodium: 42mg

Ingredients:

- 1 1/3 cups of fat-free milk

- 3 large eggs

- ¾ cup of all-purpose white flour

- 3 tbsp. of melted unsalted butter

- 2 cups of hulled and sliced fresh strawberries

Directions:

1. In a blender, add milk and eggs and pulse till combined.

2. Slowly, add flour and pulse for about 1 minute.

3. Transfer the mixture into a bowl, and keep aside, covered for about 1 hour.

4. Add melted butter and beat till well combined.

5. Heat a lightly, greased 8-inh crepe pan on medium heat.

6. Add about ¼ cup of the mixture in the pan and tilt the pan to spread it evenly.

7. Cook for about 20-25 seconds per side.

8. Repeat with the remaining mixture.

9. Serve with the strawberries.

SUPER-SIMPLE PANCAKES (9 SERVINGS, SERVING: 2 PANCAKES)

Per Serving, Calories: 168- Fat: 4.3g - Carbs: 25.3g - Protein: 5.9g - Fiber: 0.8g - Potassium: 128mg - Sodium: 198mg

Ingredients:

- 2 cups of fat-free milk

- 1 tbsp. of vinegar

- 2 cups of sifted all-purpose white flour

- 1 tbsp. of sugar

- 1 tsp. of baking soda

- Pinch of salt

- 2 eggs

- 2 tbsp. of canola oil

Directions:

1. In a bowl, mix together milk and vinegar and keep aside for about 5 minutes.

2. In a large bowl, mix together flour, sugar, baking soda and salt.

3. In another bowl, crack the eggs and beat till fluffy.

4. Add milk mixture and oil and beat till well combined.

5. Add flour mixture and beat till smooth.

6. Heat a lightly, greased nonstick skillet on medium-low heat.

7. Add about ¼ cup of mixture and tilt the pan to spread it evenly in the skillet.

8. Cook for about 2-3 minutes.

9. Carefully, flip the side and cook for about 1-2 minutes.

10. Repeat with the remaining mixture.

LIGHT PANCAKES (6 SERVINGS, SERVING: 2 PANCAKES)

Per Serving, Calories: 227- Fat: 14.2g - Carbs: 5.1g - Protein: 10.5g - Fiber: 1.7g - Potassium: 200mg - Sodium: 250mg

Ingredients:

- 1 cup of low-fat cottage cheese

- ½ cup of sifted all-purpose white flour

- 1/3 cup of melted unsalted butter

- 4 lightly beaten eggs

- 3 cups of hulled and sliced fresh strawberries

Directions:

In a bowl, add cheese, flour, butter and eggs and mix till well combined.

Heat a lightly, greased nonstick skillet on medium-high heat.

Add about ¼ cup of mixture and tilt the pan to spread it evenly in the skillet.

Cook for about 2-3 minutes.

Carefully, flip the side and cook for about 1-2 minutes.

Repeat with the remaining mixture.

Serve with the topping of strawberries.

CLASSIC BAKED PANCAKES (4 SERVINGS, SERVING: 1 PORTION)

Per Serving, Calories: 135- Fat: 6.2g - Carbs: 13.6g - Protein: 5.8g - Fiber: 0g - Potassium: 98mg - Sodium: 52mg

Ingredients:

- ½ cup of fat-free milk

- 2 large eggs

- ½ cup of all-purpose white flour

- 1/8 tsp. of ground nutmeg

- 1 tbsp. of canola oil

Directions:

1. Preheat the oven to 450 degrees F.

2. In a bowl, add milk and eggs and beat till well combined.

3. Add flour and nutmeg and mix till well combine.

4. In a 9-inchpie dish, add the oil and place in the heated oven for about 5 minutes.

5. Carefully, place the flour mixture into the pie dish evenly.

6. Bake for about 18-20 minutes.

7. Cut into 4 equal sized wedges and serve.

MOIST WAFFLES (8 SERVINGS, SERVING: 1 WAFFLE)

Per Serving, Calories: 195- Fat: 8.2g - Carbs: 26.3g - Protein: 5.2g - Fiber: 2.3g - Potassium: 99mg - Sodium: 37mg

Ingredients:

- ½ cup of warm water

- 2 envelopes of active dry yeast

- 2 cups of unsweetened brown rice milk

- ¼ cup of olive oil

- 1 tsp. of sugar

- 2 lightly beaten eggs

- 1½ cups of white flour

- ½ cup of cornmeal

Directions:

1. In a large bowl, add warm water.

2. Add yeast and stir till dissolve completely.

3. Keep aside for about 5 minutes.

4. Add rice milk, oil, and sugar and beat till well combined.

5. Add eggs, flour and cornmeal and beat till just moistened.

6. Keep in the warm place for about 15 minutes.

7. Preheat the waffle iron and then grease it.

8. In preheated waffle iron, add required amount of mixture and cook for about 4-5 minutes.

9. Repeat with the remaining mixture.

Flavored Spicy Waffles (10 servings, serving: 1 waffle)

Per Serving, Calories: 217- Fat: 8.8g - Carbs: 29g - Protein: 5.5g - Fiber: 1.5g - Potassium: 244mg - Sodium: 167mg

Ingredients:

- 1½ cups of all-purpose white flour

- 1 cup of yellow cornmeal

- 2 tbsp. of sugar

- 2 tsp. of baking powder

- 1 tsp. of baking soda

- 2 tsp. of ground cumin

- 1 tsp. of ground chipotle pepper

- 1¾ cups of fat-free milk

- 1/3 cup of vegetable oil

- 2 eggs

- 2 tbsp. of minced chives

Directions:

1. In a large bowl, mix together flour, sugar, baking powder, baking soda and spices.

2. In another bowl, add milk, oil and eggs and beat till well combined.

3. Add egg milk into flour mixture and mix till well combined.

4. Fold in chives and keep aside for about 10 minutes.

5. Preheat the waffle iron and then grease it.

6. In preheated waffle iron, add about 1/3 cup of mixture and cook for about 4-5 minutes.

7. Repeat with the remaining mixture.

NUTRITIOUS OATMEAL (3 SERVINGS, SERVING: 1 PORTION)

Per Serving, Calories: 178- Fat: 5.9g - Carbs: 25.3g - Protein: 7.4g - Fiber: 4.4g - Potassium: 263mg - Sodium: 109mg

Ingredients:

- ¾ cup of quick-cooking oatmeal

- 1 cup of unsweetened almond milk

- 2 large eggs

- 1 medium apple, cored and chopped finely

- ½ tsp. of ground cinnamon

Directions:

In a large bowl, add oatmeal, almond milk and eggs and with a fork, mix well.

Add apple and cinnamon and mix till well combined.

Divide the mixture in 2 microwave safe large mugs evenly.

Microwave on High for about 2 minutes.

Remove the mugs from the microwave and fluff with a fork.

Microwave on High for about 30-60 seconds more.

CHAPTER 2: LUNCH RECIPES

ENERGETIC FRUITY SALAD (12 SERVINGS, SERVING: 1 SALAD PLATE)

Per Serving, Calories: 116- Fat: 0.5g - Carbs: 29.3g - Protein: 1.2g - Fiber: 5.3g - Potassium: 276mg - Sodium: 3mg

Ingredients:

For Dressing:

- ½ cup of fresh pineapple juice

- 2 tbsp. of fresh lemon juice

For Salad:

- 2 cups of hulled and sliced fresh strawberries

- 2 cups of fresh blackberries

- 2 cups of fresh blueberries

- 1 cup of halved seedless red grapes

- 1 cup of halved seedless red grapes

- 6 cored and chopped fresh apples

Directions:

1. In a bowl, add all dressing ingredients and beat till well combined. Keep aside.

2. In another large bowl, mix together all salad ingredients.

3. Add dressing and gently, toss to coat well.

4. Refrigerate, covered to chill before serving.

APPEALING GREEN SALAD (4 SERVINGS, SERVING: 1 SALAD PLATE)

Per Serving, Calories: 179- Fat: 17.1g - Carbs: 7.5g - Protein: 1.7g - Fiber: 1.9g - Potassium: 249mg - Sodium: 21mg

Ingredients:

For Dressing:

- 1 tbsp. of shallot, minced

- 1/3 cup of olive oil

- 2 tbsp. of fresh lemon juice

- 1 tsp. of honey

- Freshly ground black pepper, to taste

For Salad:

- 1½ cups of chopped broccoli florets

- 1½ cups of shredded cabbage

- 4 cups of chopped lettuce

Directions:

1. In a bowl, add all dressing ingredients and beat till well combined. Keep aside.

2. In another large bowl, mix together all salad ingredients.

3. Add dressing and gently, toss to coat well.

4. Serve immediately.

GARDEN FRESH SALAD (6 SERVINGS, SERVING: 1 SALAD PLATE)

Per Serving, Calories: 71- Fat: 17.1g - Carbs: 7.2g - Protein: 1.1g - Fiber: 2.2g - Potassium: 247mg - Sodium: 63mg

Ingredients:

For Salad:

- 2 cups of peeled and shredded carrots

- 1½ cups of shredded green cabbage

- 1½ cups of shredded purple cabbage

- 1 cup of chopped cucumber

- 2 chopped large scallions

- ¼ cup of chopped fresh parsley leaves

For Dressing:

- 2 tbsp. of olive oil

- 2 tbsp. of fresh lemon juice

- 1 tsp. of finely grated fresh lemon zest

- Pinch of salt

- Freshly ground black pepper, to taste

Directions:

1. In a large serving bowl, add all salad ingredients

2. In another bowl, all dressing ingredients and mix till well combined.

3. Pour dressing over salad and toss to coat well. Serve immediately.

SOPHISTICATED SALAD (6 SERVINGS, SERVING: 1 SALAD PLATE)

Per Serving, Calories: 235- Fat: 17.1g - Carbs: 19.8g - Protein: 1.2g - Fiber: 4g - Potassium: 231mg - Sodium: 35mg

Ingredients:

For Dressing:

- ½ cup of olive oil

- ¼ cup of fresh lemon juice

- 2 tbsp. of sugar

- 1 minced garlic clove

- Freshly ground black pepper, to taste

For Salad:

- 2 medium cored and chopped apples

- ½ of chopped medium cabbage head

- ½ cup of dried cranberries

- ¼ cup of chopped red onion

Directions:

1. In a bowl, add all dressing ingredients and beat till well combined. Keep aside.

2. In another large bowl, mix together all salad ingredients.

3. Add dressing and gently, toss to coat well. Serve immediately.

AROMATIC CUCUMBER SOUP (2 SERVINGS, SERVING: 1 BOWL)

Per Serving, Calories: 33- Fat: 1.9g - Carbs: 3.9g - Protein: 1.2g - Fiber: 1.2g - Potassium: 227mg - Sodium: 96mg

Ingredients:

- 1 cup of peeled and chopped cucumber

- 1 chopped scallion

- 2 tbsp. of fresh parsley leaves

- 2 tbsp. of fresh basil leaves

- ¼ tsp. of finely grated fresh lemon zest

- 1 cup of unsweetened almond milk

- ¼ cup of water

- ½ tbsp. of fresh lemon juice

Directions:

1. In a blender, add all ingredients and pulse till smooth.

2. Transfer the soup into a large bowl and refrigerate, covered for about 4-6 hours.

3. Serve chilled.

BRIGHT GREEN BROCCOLI SOUP (5 SERVINGS, SERVING: 1 BOWL)

Per Serving, Calories: 66- Fat: 3.1g - Carbs: 7g - Protein: 3.5g - Fiber: 2.3g - Potassium: 243mg - Sodium: 73mg

Ingredients:

- 1 tbsp. of canola oil

- ½ cup of chopped onion

- 1 minced garlic clove

- 1 tbsp. of chopped fresh thyme

- ¼ tsp. of ground cumin

- ¼ tsp. of crushed red pepper flakes

- ¾ pound of broccoli florets

- 3½ cups of low-sodium vegetable broth, divided

Directions:

1. In a large soup pan, heat oil on medium heat.

2. Add onion and sauté for about 4-5 minutes.

3. Add garlic, thyme and spices and sauté for about 1 minute.

4. Add broccoli and cook for about 3-4 minutes.

5. Add broth and bring to a boil on high heat.

6. Reduce the heat to medium-low and simmer, covered for about 30-35 minutes.

7. Remove from heat and keep aside to cool slightly.

8. Transfer the mixture in a high speed blender in batches and pulse till smooth.

9. Serve immediately.

HEALTHY SOUP (6 SERVINGS, SERVING: 1 BOWL)

Per Serving, Calories: 111- Fat: 6.7g - Carbs: 7.1g - Protein: 5.8g - Fiber: 1.6g - Potassium: 225mg - Sodium: 142mg

Ingredients:

- 2 cups of chopped cauliflower florets

- ½ cup of peeled and chopped carrot

- 1 cup of chopped onion

- 2 minced garlic cloves

- 4½ cups of low-sodium vegetable broth

- Freshly ground black pepper, to taste

- 2-ounce of shredded low-fat cheddar cheese, shredded

- ¾ cup of half-and-half creamer

- ¼ cup of chopped fresh parsley

Directions:

1. In a large soup pan, mix together cauliflower, carrot, onion, garlic, broth and black pepper on medium-high heat and bring to a boil.

2. Reduce the heat to low and simmer for about 10 minutes.

3. Remove from heat and keep aside to cool slightly.

4. In a large blender, add soup in batches and pulse till smooth.

5. Return the soup into pan on medium-low heat.

6. Stir in cheese and half-and-half and simmer for about 2-3
    minutes or till heated completely.

7. Serve hot with the garnishing of basil.

SUPERB LUNCHEON SOUP (5 SERVINGS, SERVING: 1 BOWL)

Per Serving, Calories: 87- Fat: 5g - Carbs: 7.7g - Protein: 3.7g - Fiber: 1.8g - Potassium: 255mg - Sodium: 85mg

Ingredients:

- 1½ tbsp. of olive oil

- 2 chopped medium onions

- 2 minced garlic cloves

- ½ tbsp. of crushed dried thyme

- 3 cups of cubed yellow squash

- 3½ cups of low-sodium vegetable broth

- 2 tbsp. of fresh lemon juice

- Freshly ground black pepper, to taste

- 2 tbsp. of shredded low-fat parmesan cheese

Directions:

1. In a large soup pan, heat oil on medium heat.

2. Add onions and sauté for about 5 minutes.

3. Add garlic and thyme and sauté for about 1 minute.

4. Add squash and cook for about 5 minutes

5. Add broth and bring to a boil.

6. Reduce the heat to low and simmer, covered for about 15-20 minutes or till desired thickness.

7. Remove from heat and keep aside to cool slightly.

8. In a large blender, add soup in batches and pulse till smooth.

9. Return the soup into pan on medium heat.

10. Stir in lemon juice and black pepper and cook for about 3-4 minutes or heated completely.

11. Serve hot with the garnishing of cheese.

EXCELLENT VEGGIE SANDWICHES (8 SERVINGS, SERVING: ½ SANDWICH)

Per Serving, Calories: 92- Fat: 5.3g - Carbs: 10.5g - Protein: 1.2g - Fiber: 0.8g - Potassium: 112mg -Sodium: 168mg

Ingredients:

- 1 sliced large tomato

- ½ of sliced cucumber

- ½ cup of thinly sliced red onion

- 1 cup of chopped romaine lettuce leaves

- ½ cup of low-sodium mayonnaise

- 8 toasted white bread slices

Directions:

1. In a large bowl, mix together tomato, cucumber, onion and lettuce.

2. Spread mayonnaise over each slice evenly.

3. Divide tomato mixture over 4 slices evenly.

4. Cover with remaining slices.

5. With a knife, carefully cut the sandwiches diagonally and serve.

LUNCHTIME STAPLE SANDWICHES (2 SERVINGS, SERVING: ½ SANDWICH)

Per Serving, Calories: 239- Fat: 8.5g - Carbs: 37.2g - Protein: 7g - Fiber: 5.6g - Potassium: 294mg - Sodium: 169mg

Ingredients:

- 3 tsp. of low-sodium mayonnaise

- 2 toasted white bread slices

- 3 tbsp. of chopped unsalted cooked turkey

- 2 thin apple slices

- 2 tbsp. of low-fat cheddar cheese

- 1 tsp. of olive oil

Directions:

1. Spread mayonnaise over each slice evenly.

2. Place turkey over 1 slice, followed by apple slices and cheese.

3. Cover with remaining slice to make sandwich.

4. Grease a large nonstick frying pan with oil and heat on medium heat.

5. Place the sandwich in frying pan and with the back of spoon, gently, press down.

6. Cook for about 1-2 minutes.

7. Carefully, flip the whole sandwich and cook for about 1-2 minutes.

8. Transfer the sandwich into serving plate.

9. With a knife, carefully cut the sandwich diagonally ad serve.

GREEK STYLE PITA ROLLS (4 SERVINGS, SERVING: ½ ROLL)

Per Serving, Calories: 129- Fat: 2.2g - Carbs: 24.6g - Protein: 3.3g - Fiber: 2.1g - Potassium: 102mg - Sodium: 176mg

Ingredients:

- 2 (6½-inch) pita breads

- 1 tbsp. of low-fat cream cheese

- 1 peeled, cored and thinly sliced apple

- Olive oil cooking spray, as required

- 1/8 tsp. of ground cinnamon

Directions:

1. Preheat the oven to 400 degrees F.

2. In a microwave safe plate, place tortillas and microwave for about 10 seconds to soften.

3. Spread the cream cheese over each tortilla evenly.

4. Arrange apple slices in the center of each tortilla evenly.

5. Roll tortillas to secure the filling.

6. Arrange the tortilla rolls onto a baking sheet in a single layer.

7. Spray the rolls with cooking spray evenly and sprinkle with cinnamon.

8. Bake for about 10 minutes or until top becomes golden brown.

HEALTHIER PITA VEGGIE ROLLS (6 SERVINGS, SERVING: ½ ROLL)

Per Serving, Calories: 120- Fat: 2.8g - Carbs: 20.7g - Protein: 3.3g - Fiber: 1.5g - Potassium: 156mg - Sodium: 164mg

Ingredients:

- 1 cup of shredded romaine lettuce

- 1 seeded and chopped red bell pepper

- ½ cup of chopped cucumber

- 1 small seeded and chopped tomato

- 1 small chopped red onion

- 1 finely minced garlic clove

- 1 tbsp. of olive oil

- ½ tbsp. of fresh lemon juice

- Freshly ground black pepper, to taste

- 3 (6½-inch) pita breads

Directions:

1. In a large bowl, add all ingredients except pita breads and gently toss to coat well.

2. Arrange pita breads onto serving plates.

3. Place veggie mixture in the center of each pita bread evenly. Roll the pita bread and serve.

CRUNCHY VEGGIE WRAPS (6 SERVINGS, SERVING: 1 WRAP)

Per Serving, Calories: 42- Fat: 3.1g - Carbs: 2.9g - Protein: 1.6g - Fiber: 1.1g - Potassium: 106mg - Sodium: 10mg

Ingredients:

- ¾ cup of shredded purple cabbage

- ¾ cup of shredded green cabbage

- ½ cup of peeled and julienned cucumber

- ½ cup of peeled and julienned carrot

- ¼ cup of chopped walnuts

- 2 tbsp. of olive oil

- 1 tbsp. of fresh lemon juice

- Pinch of salt

- Freshly ground black pepper, to taste

- 6 medium butter lettuce leaves

Directions:

1. In a large bowl, add all ingredients except lettuce and toss to coat well.

2. Place the lettuce leaves onto serving plates.

3. Divide the veggie mixture over each leaf evenly. Top with tofu sauce and serve.

SURPRISINGLY TASTY CHICKEN WRAPS (4 SERVINGS, SERVING: 1 WRAP)

Per Serving, Calories: 74- Fat: 2.3g - Carbs: 4.7g - Protein: 8.9g - Fiber: 0.9g - Potassium: 235mg - Sodium: 27mg

Ingredients:

- 4-ounce of cut into strips unsalted cooked chicken breast

- ½ cup of hulled and thinly sliced fresh strawberries

- 1 thinly sliced English cucumber

- 1 tbsp. of chopped fresh mint leaves

- 4 large lettuce leaves

Directions:

1. In a large bowl, add all ingredients except lettuce leaves and gently toss to coat well.

2. Place the lettuce leaves onto serving plates.

3. Divide the chicken mixture over each leaf evenly.

4. Serve immediately.

AUTHENTIC SHRIMP WRAPS (4 SERVINGS, SERVING: 1 WRAP)

Per Serving, Calories: 97- Fat: 4.3g - Carbs: 3g - Protein: 12.6g - Fiber: 0.5g - Potassium: 81mg - Sodium: 169mg

Ingredients:

For Filling:

- 1 tbsp. of olive oil

- 1 minced garlic clove

- 1 seeded and chopped medium red bell pepper

- ½ pound of peeled, deveined and chopped medium shrimp

- Pinch of salt

- Freshly ground black pepper, to taste

For Wraps:

- 4 large lettuce leaves

Directions:

1. In a large skillet, heat oil on medium heat.

2. Add garlic and sauté for about 30 seconds.

3. Add bell pepper and cook for about 2-3 minutes.

4. Add shrimp and seasoning and cook for about 2-3 minutes.

5. Remove from heat and cool slightly. Divide shrimp mixture over lettuce leaves evenly. Serve immediately.

LOVEABLE TORTILLAS (8 SERVINGS, SERVING: ½ TORTILLA)

Per Serving, Calories: 296- Fat: 8.2g - Carbs: 44g - Protein: 13.5g - Fiber: 5.9g - Potassium: 262mg - Sodium: 162mg

Ingredients:

- ½ cup of low-sodium mayonnaise

- 1 finely minced small garlic clove

- 8-ounce of chopped unsalted cooked chicken

- ½ of seeded and chopped red bell pepper

- ½ of seeded and chopped green bell pepper

- 1 chopped red onion

- 4 (6-ounce) warmed corn tortillas

Directions:

1. In a bowl, mix together mayonnaise and garlic.

2. In another bowl, mix together chicken and vegetables.

3. Arrange the tortillas onto smooth surface.

4. Spread mayonnaise mixture over each tortilla evenly.

5. Place chicken mixture over ¼ of each tortilla.

6. Fold the outside edges inward and roll up like a burrito.

7. Secure each tortilla with toothpicks to secure the filling.

8. Cut each tortilla in half and serve.

ELEGANT VEGGIE TORTILLAS (12 SERVINGS, SERVING: ½ TORTILLA)

Per Serving, Calories: 217- Fat: 3.3g - Carbs: 41g - Protein: 8.1g - Fiber: 6.3g - Potassium: 289mg - Sodium: 87mg

Ingredients:

- 1½ cups of chopped broccoli florets

- 1½ cups of chopped cauliflower florets

- 1 tbsp. of water

- 2 tsp. of canola oil

- 1½ cups of chopped onion

- 1 minced garlic clove

- 2 tbsp. of finely chopped fresh parsley

- 1 cup of low-cholesterol liquid egg substitute

- Freshly ground black pepper, to taste

- 4 (6-ounce) warmed corn tortillas

Directions:

1. In a microwave bowl, place broccoli, cauliflower and water and microwave, covered for about 3-5 minutes.

2. Remove from microwave and drain any liquid.

3. In a skillet, heat oil on medium heat.

4. Add onion and sauté for about 4-5 minutes.

5. Add garlic and sauté for about 1 minute.

6. Stir in broccoli, cauliflower, parsley, egg substitute and black pepper.

7. Reduce the heat to medium-low and simmer for about 10 minutes.

8. Remove from heat and keep aside to cool slightly.

9. Place broccoli mixture over ¼ of each tortilla.

10. Fold the outside edges inward and roll up like a burrito.

11. Secure each tortilla with toothpicks to secure the filling.

12. Cut each tortilla in half and serve.

DELIGHTFUL PIZZA (4 SERVINGS, SERVING: ½ PIZZA)

Per Serving, Calories: 133- Fat: 2g - Carbs: 18.2g - Protein: 9.8g - Fiber: 1g - Potassium: mg - Sodium: 287mg

Ingredients:

- 2 (6½-inch) pita breads

- 3 tbsp. of low-sodium tomato sauce

- 3-ounce of cubed unsalted cooked chicken

- ¼ cup of chopped onion

- 2 tbsp. of crumbled feta cheese

Directions:

1. Preheat the oven to 350 degrees F. Grease a baking sheet.

2. Arrange the pita breads onto prepared baking sheet.

3. Spread the barbecue sauce over each pita bread evenly.

4. Top with chicken and onion evenly and sprinkle with cheese.

5. Bake for about 11-13 minutes.

6. Cut each pizza in half and serve.

Luxurious Pizza (4 servings, serving: ½ pizza)

Per Serving, Calories: 104 - Fat: 5.8g - Carbs: 7.1g - Protein: 6.3g - Fiber: 1.1g - Potassium: 108mg - Sodium: 62mg

Ingredients:

- 2 (8-inch) flour tortillas

- Olive oil cooking spray, as required

- 2-ounce of softened low-fat cream cheese

- 3 tbsp. of low-sodium marinara sauce

- 2-ounce of chopped unsalted grilled chicken

- ¼ cup of chopped broccoli

- ¼ cup of sliced fresh mushrooms

- ¼ cup of sliced red onion

Directions:

1. Preheat the oven to 400 degrees F. Line a baking sheet with a piece of foil.

2. Spray the both sides of tortillas with cooking spray evenly.

3. Arrange the tortillas onto prepared baking sheet.

4. Bake for about 5-10 minutes or till golden brown from both sides, flipping as required.

5. Remove the tortillas from the oven.

6. Spread cream cheese over both tortillas evenly, followed by marinara sauce.

7. Top with turkey, followed by broccoli, mushrooms and onion evenly.

8. Bake for about 5 minutes.

9. Cut each tortilla in half and serve.

WINNER KABOBS (6 SERVINGS, SERVING: 1 SKEWER)

Per Serving, Calories: 182- Fat: 3g - Carbs: 22.2g - Protein: 18g - Fiber: 2.3g - Potassium: 234mg - Sodium: 185mg

Ingredients:

- 1 pound of cubed skinless, boneless chicken breast

- 1 seeded and cut into 1-inch pieces medium red bell pepper

- 1 seeded and cut into 1-inch pieces medium green bell pepper

- 20-ounce of cut into 1-inch pieces pineapple

- 1 cut into 1-inch pieces red onion

- 1/3 cup of low-sodium barbecue sauce

- Freshly ground black pepper, to taste

Directions:

1. Preheat the outdoor grill to medium-high heat. Lightly, grease the grill grate.

2. Thread chicken, bell peppers, pineapple and onion onto pre-soaked 6 wooden skewers.

3. Coat all the ingredients with ½ of barbecue sauce and sprinkle with black pepper.

4. Place the skewers in prepared baking sheet in a single layer.

5. Grill the skewers for about 9-10 minutes, flipping occasionally.

6. Remove from grill and immediately, coat with remaining barbecue sauce. Serve immediately.

TEMPTING BURGERS (6 SERVINGS, SERVING: 2 BURGERS WITH ½ CUP LETTUCE)

Per Serving, Calories: 136- Fat: 9.1g - Carbs: 2.1g - Protein: 12.4g - Fiber: 0.5g - Potassium: 295mg - Sodium: 39mg

Ingredients:

- 12-ounce of finely chopped unsalted cooked salmon

- ½ cup of minced onion

- 1 minced garlic clove

- 2 tbsp. of chopped fresh parsley

- 1 large egg

- ½ tsp. of paprika

- Freshly ground black pepper, to taste

- 2 tbsp. of olive oil

- 3 cups torn lettuce

Directions:

1. Preheat the oven to 350 degrees F. Line a baking sheet with parchment paper.

2. In a large bowl, add all ingredients except oil and mix till well combined.

3. Make equal sized 12 patties from mixture.

4. Place patties onto prepared baking dish in a single layer.

5. Bake for about 12-15 minutes.

6. Now, in a large skillet, heat oil on high heat.

7. Remove salmon burgers from oven and transfer into skillet.

8. Cook for about 1 minute per side.

9. Divide lettuce in serving plates evenly.

10. Place 2 patties in each plate and serve.

TASTIEST MEATBALLS (6 SERVINGS, SERVING: 3-4 MEATBALLS WITH ½ CUP LETTUCE)

Per Serving, Calories: 126- Fat: 6.5 g - Carbs: 1.2g - Protein: 15.5g - Fiber: 0.5g - Potassium: 49mg - Sodium: 85mg

Ingredients:

- 1 pound of lean ground chicken

- 1 tbsp. of olive oil

- 1 tsp. of minced garlic

- 2 tbsp. of minced fresh cilantro

- ½ tsp. of ground cumin

- ½ tsp. of crushed red pepper flakes

- 3 cups of torn lettuce leaves

Directions:

1. Preheat the oven to 400 degrees F.

2. Line a large baking sheet with parchment paper.

3. For meatballs in a large bowl, add all ingredients and mix till well combined.

4. Make desired sized balls from mixture.

5. Arrange the meatballs into prepared baking sheet in a single layer.

6. Bake for about 15-20 minutes or till done completely.

7. Divide lettuce in serving plates evenly. Top with meatballs and serve.

TANGY MUSHROOM STIR-FRY (4 SERVINGS, SERVING: 1 PORTION)

Per Serving, Calories: 48- Fat: 2.6g - Carbs: 5.3g - Protein: 2.2g - Fiber: 0.6g – Potassium: 244mg – Sodium: 7mg

Ingredients:

- 2 tsp. of olive oil

- ½ cup of chopped shallots

- 3 cups of sliced fresh button mushrooms

- Freshly ground black pepper, to taste

- 2 tbsp. of fresh lemon juice

Directions:

1. In a large skillet, heat oil on medium heat.

2. Add shallot and sauté for about 2-3 minutes.

3. Add mushrooms and black pepper and cook for about 5-7 minutes or till mushrooms become tender.

4. Stir in lemon juice and remove from heat.

5. Serve immediately.

SIMPLE BROCCOLI STIR-FRY (4 SERVINGS, SERVING: 1 PORTION)

Per Serving, Calories: 47- Fat: 3.6g - Carbs: 3.3g - Protein: 1.3g - Fiber: 1.2g - Potassium: 147mg - Sodium: 15mg

Ingredients:

- 1 tbsp. of olive oil

- 1 minced garlic clove

- 2 cups of broccoli florets

- 2 tbsp. of water

Directions:

In a large skillet, heat oil on medium heat.

Add garlic and sauté for about 1 minute.

Add broccoli and stir fry for about 2 minutes.

Stir in water and stir fry for about 4-5 minutes.

Serve warm.

BRAISED CABBAGE (4 SERVINGS, SERVING: 1 PORTION)

Per Serving, Calories: 45- Fat: 1.8g - Carbs: 6.6g - Protein: 1.1g - Fiber: 1.9g - Potassium: 136mg - Sodium: 46mg

Ingredients:

- 1½ tsp. of olive oil

- 2 minced garlic cloves

- 1 thinly sliced onion

- 3 cups of chopped green cabbage

- 1 cup of low- sodium vegetable broth

- Freshly ground black pepper, to taste

Directions:

1. In a large skillet, heat oil on medium-high heat.

2. Add garlic and sauté for about 1 minute.

3. Add onion and sauté for about 4-5 minutes.

4. Add cabbage and sauté for about 3-4 minutes.

5. Stir in broth and black pepper and immediately, reduce the heat to low.

6. Cook, covered for about 20 minutes.

7. Serve warm.

PERFECT ZUCCHINI STIR-FRY (5 SERVINGS, SERVING: 1 PORTION)

Per Serving, Calories: 41- Fat: 3g - Carbs: 3.3g - Protein: 1.2g - Fiber: 1.1g – Potassium: 246mg – Sodium: 10mg

Ingredients:

- 1 tbsp. of canola oil

- 1 pound thickly sliced zucchinis

- 1 minced garlic clove

- 1 tbsp. of fresh lemon juice

- Freshly ground black pepper, to taste

- 1 tsp. of minced fresh mint leaves

Directions:

1. In a large skillet, heat oil on medium-high heat.

2. Add zucchini and garlic and stir fry for about 2-3 minutes

3. Add lemon juice and black pepper and stir fry for about 2 minutes.

4. Stir in mint and cook for about 1-2 minutes.

5. Serve hot.

NUTRIENT DENSE LUNCH MEAL (5 SERVINGS, SERVING: 1 PORTION)

Per Serving, Calories: 91- Fat: 3.1g - Carbs: 16.4g - Protein: 1.6g - Fiber: 3.5g - Potassium: 245mg - Sodium: 21mg

Ingredients:

- 1 tbsp. of olive oil

- 2 minced garlic cloves

- 2 cups of broccoli florets

- ½ cup of chopped red onion

- ¼ cup of chopped celery stalk

- ¼ cup of low-sodium vegetable broth

- 2 cored and sliced apples

Directions:

1. In a large skillet, heat oil on medium-high heat.

2. Add garlic and sauté for about 30 seconds.

3. Add broccoli and stir fry for about 4-5 minutes.

4. Add celery and onion and stir fry for about 4-5 minutes.

5. Stir in broth and cook for about 2-3 minutes.

6. Stir in apple slices and cook for about 2-3 minutes.

7. Serve hot.

COLORFUL VEGGIE SKILLET (5 SERVINGS, SERVING: 1 PORTION)

Per Serving, Calories: 50- Fat: 3g - Carbs: 5.5g - Protein: 1.3g - Fiber: 1.4g - Potassium: 243mg - Sodium: 11mg

Ingredients:

- 1 tbsp. of canola oil

- ½ cup of sliced onion

- ½ cup of seeded and julienned red bell pepper

- ½ cup of seeded and julienned green bell pepper

- 3 cups of sliced yellow squash

- 1½ tsp. of minced garlic

- ¼ cup of low-sodium vegetable broth

- Freshly ground black pepper, to taste

Directions:

1. In a large skillet, heat oil on medium-high heat.

2. Add onion, bell peppers and squash and sauté for about 4-5 minutes.

3. Add garlic and sauté for about 1 minute.

4. Stir in remaining ingredients and reduce the heat to medium.

5. Cook for about 3-4 minutes, stirring occasionally.

IMPRESSIVE BAKED VEGGIES (5 SERVINGS, SERVING: 1 PORTION)

Per Serving, Calories: 87- Fat: 7g - Carbs: 4g - Protein: 3.2g - Fiber: 1.1g - Potassium: 256mg - Sodium: 65mg

Ingredients:

- 2 minced garlic cloves

- ½ of seeded and minced small jalapeño pepper

- ¼ cup of low-sodium vegetable broth

- 2 tbsp. of canola oil

- ½ tsp. of ground cumin

- ¼ tsp. of paprika

- ½ pound of sliced crosswise zucchini

- ½ pound of sliced crosswise yellow squash

- 1 tbsp. of fresh lemon juice

- ¼ cup of grated low-fat Parmesan cheese

Directions:

1. Preheat the oven to 355 degrees F.

2. In a large mixing bowl, mix together all ingredients except zucchini and lemon juice.

3. Add zucchini slices and coat with garlic mixture generously.

4. Place zucchini slices in a shallow baking dish.

5. Pour remaining mixture over zucchini evenly.

6. Cover the baking dish and bake for about 15 minutes.

7. Remove from the oven and stir the zucchini slices with mixture completely.

8. Bake, uncovered for about 5-10 minutes more.

9. Remove from the oven and sprinkle with cheese.

10. Immediately, cover the baking dish and keep aside for about 5 minutes before serving.

DECADENT CAULIFLOWER (6 SERVINGS, SERVING: 1 PORTION)

Per Serving, Calories: 107- Fat: 9.7g - Carbs: 3g - Protein: 3.2g - Fiber: 1.1g - Potassium: 136mg - Sodium: 143mg

Ingredients:

- 1 head of cauliflower

- 2 tsp. of low-sodium mayonnaise

- ¼ cup of chopped unsalted butter

- 1/3 cup of grated low-fat Parmesan cheese

Directions:

1. In a large pan of boiling water, place steamer basket.

2. Place the cauliflower in steamer basket and steam, covered for about 30 minutes.

3. Drain well.

4. Preheat the oven to 375 degrees F.

5. Spread mayonnaise over cauliflower head evenly.

6. Arrange cauliflower head in a baking dish.

7. Top the cauliflower with the butter in the shape of dots.

8. Sprinkle with cheese evenly.

9. Bake for about 30 minutes.

QUICKER SHRIMP STIR-FRY (3 SERVINGS, SERVING: 1 PORTION)

Per Serving, Calories: 134 - Fat: 6g - Carbs: 2g - Protein: 17.4g - Fiber: 0g - Potassium: 146mg - Sodium: 185mg

Ingredients:

- 1 tbsp. of olive oil

- 2 minced garlic cloves

- 1 seeded and finely chopped Serrano pepper

- ½ pound of peeled and deveined shrimp

- 1 tsp. of fresh lemon juice

- 1 tbsp. of chopped fresh cilantro

Directions:

1. In a large skillet, heat oil on medium heat.

2. Add garlic and Serrano pepper and sauté for about 1 minute.

3. Add shrimp and cook for about 4-5 minutes or till done completely.

4. Stir in lemon juice and remove from heat.

5. Serve hot with the topping of cilantro.

ZESTY PILAF (8 SERVINGS, SERVING: 1 PORTION)

Per Serving, Calories: 232- Fat: 5.4g - Carbs: 39.3g - Protein: 5.4g - Fiber: 1g - Potassium: 98mg - Sodium: 111mg

Ingredients:

- 3 tbsp. of unsalted margarine

- 1 cup of chopped onion

- 1 finely chopped garlic clove

- 2 cups of long-grain white rice

- ¼ cup grated low-fat Parmesan cheese

- ¼ cup of chopped fresh parsley

- ¼ cup of fresh lemon juice

- Freshly ground black pepper, to taste

- 2¾ cups of hot low-sodium vegetable broth

Directions:

1. Preheat the oven to 350 degrees F.

2. In a Dutch oven, melt margarine on medium heat.

3. Add onion and garlic and sauté for about 2-3 minutes.

4. Add rice and sauté for about 2 minutes.

5. Stir in cheese, parsley, lemon juice and black pepper.

6. Add hot broth and stir to combine.

7. Cover the pan and transfer into the oven.

8. Bake for about 20 minutes.

VERSATILE PILAF (8 SERVINGS, SERVING: 1 PORTION)

Per Serving, Calories: 220- Fat: 4.9g - Carbs: 37.8g - Protein: 5.2g - Fiber: 1.4g - Potassium: 50mg - Sodium: 69mg

Ingredients:

- 3 tbsp. of unsalted margarine
- 1/3 cup of chopped celery
- 1/3 cup of chopped onion
- 1 cup of white rice
- 1 cup of broken into small pieces vermicelli
- 1½ cups of water
- 1½ cups of low-sodium vegetable broth
- 1 tbsp. of chopped fresh parsley

Directions:

1. In a large skillet, melt the margarine on medium heat.
2. Add celery and onion and sauté for about 1-2 minutes.
3. Add rice and vermicelli and stir fry for about 30 seconds.
4. Add water, broth and parsley and bring to a boil.
5. Reduce the heat and simmer, covered fr about 15 minutes or till all the liquid is absorbed.

Unique Rice Platter (6 servings, serving: 1 portion)

Per Serving, Calories: 198- Fat: 9.3g - Carbs: 25.8g - Protein: 2.4g - Fiber: 0.7g – Potassium: 80mg – Sodium: 59mg

Ingredients:

- ¼ cup of canola oil

- ¼ cup of chopped onion

- 1 minced garlic clove

- 1 cup of white rice

- 3 cups of water

- ¼ cup of low-sodium tomato sauce

- Freshly ground black pepper, to taste

Directions:

1. In a large pan, heat oil on medium-high heat.

2. Add bell pepper, onion celery and sauté for about 4-5 minutes.

3. Add rice and stir fry for about 2 minutes.

4. Stir in remaining ingredients.

5. Reduce the heat and simmer, covered for about 20 minutes or till all the liquid is absorbed.

LEMONY PASTA (3 SERVINGS, SERVING: 1 PORTION)

Per Serving, Calories: 153- Fat: 5.6g - Carbs: 21.6g - Protein: 4.3g - Fiber: 0.6g - Potassium: 130mg - Sodium: 16mg

Ingredients:

- 1 tbsp. of olive oil

- 1/3 cup of seeded and chopped bell pepper

- ¼ cup of chopped onion

- 2 tbsp. of chopped celery

- ¾ cup of cooked hot pasta

- ½ tsp. of crushed dried oregano

- 1 tsp. of finely grated fresh lemon zest

- 2 tbsp. of fresh lemon juice

- Freshly ground black pepper, to taste

Directions:

1. In a large pan, melt the butter on medium heat.

2. Add bell pepper, onion celery and sauté for about 4-5 minutes.

3. Add remaining ingredients and stir to combine well.

4. Serve immediately.

CHAPTER 3: DINNER RECIPES

ALL-IN-ONE SALAD (16 SERVINGS, SERVING: 1 SALAD PLATE)

Per Serving, Calories: 341- Fat: 13.7g - Carbs: 44.3g - Protein: 10.8g - Fiber: 1.9g - Potassium: 290mg - Sodium: 91mg

Ingredients:

For Dressing:

- 3 minced garlic cloves

- ¼ cup of chopped fresh parsley

- 1 cup of olive oil

- ½ cup of fresh lemon juice

- ½ tsp. of crushed dried oregano

- ½ tsp. of crushed dried basil

- Pinch of salt

- Freshly ground black pepper, to taste

For Salad:

- 1 pound of cooked shrimp

- 4 cups of cooked white rice

- 3 cups of seeded and chopped bell peppers

- 2 cups of chopped cucumber

- 1 cup of chopped red onion

- 8-ounce of chopped pineapple

- ½ cup of dried cranberries

- ½ cup of minced fresh parsley

- 1/3 cup of minced fresh dill weed

- 8 cups of torn lettuce

Directions:

1. In a bowl, add all dressing ingredients and beat till well combined. Keep aside.

2. In another large bowl, mix together all salad ingredients except lettuce.

3. Add dressing and gently, toss to coat well.

4. Refrigerate, covered to chill completely.

5. Divide the lettuce into serving plates evenly.

6. Top with salad and serve.

Entrée Salmon Salad (8 servings, serving: 1 salad plate)

Per Serving, Calories: 151 - Fat: 12.7g - Carbs: 6g - Protein: 5.5g - Fiber: 2.8g - Potassium: 274mg - Sodium: 18mg

Ingredients:

For Salad:

- 1 pound of trimmed and cut into 1-inch pieces fresh asparagus

- ¼ pound of chopped unsalted cooked salmon

- ½ cup f thawed frozen peas

- 6 cups of torn lettuce

- ½ cup pecans, toasted and chopped

For Dressing:

- ¼ cup of olive oil

- 2 tbsp. of fresh lemon juice

- Pinch of salt

- Freshly ground black pepper, to taste

Directions:

1. In a pan of boiling water, add asparagus and cook for about 5 minutes. Drain well.

2. In a large bowl, add asparagus and remaining salad ingredients.

3. In another bowl, add all dressing ingredients and beat till well combined.

4. Pour dressing over salad and gently, toss to coat well. Serve immediately.

EYE-CATCHING SALAD (8 SERVINGS, SERVING: 1 SALAD PLATE)

Per Serving, Calories: 225 - Fat: 8.7g - Carbs: 21.1g - Protein: 17g - Fiber: 3.6g - Potassium: 386mg - Sodium: 107mg

Ingredients:

- 4 tsp. fresh lemon juice, divided

- 1½ tbsp. olive oil, divided

- Pinch of salt

- Freshly ground black pepper, to taste

- 1 pound of trimmed flank steak

- Cooking spray, as required

- 1 tsp. honey

- 4 cups torn lettuce

- 5 cored and thinly sliced apples

- ¼ cup feta cheese, crumbled

Directions:

1. In a large bowl, mix together 1 tsp. of lemon juice, 1½ tsp. of extra-virgin olive oil, salt and black pepper.

2. Add steak and coat with mixture generously.

3. Grease a nonstick skillet with a little cooking spray and heat on medium high-heat.

4. Add beef steak and cook for 5-6 minutes per side.

5. Transfer the steak onto a cutting board and keep aside for about 10 minutes before slicing.

6. With a sharp knife, cut the beef steak diagonally across grain in desired size slices.

7. In a large bowl, add remaining lemon juice, oil, honey, pinch of salt and black pepper and beat well.

8. Add lettuce and toss well. Divide lettuce in 4 serving plates.

9. Top with beef slices, apple slices and cheese evenly and serve.

FILLING CHICKEN SOUP (5 SERVINGS, SERVING: 1 BOWL)

Per Serving, Calories: 98- Fat: 3.8g - Carbs: 4.4g - Protein: 11g - Fiber: 1g - Potassium: 229mg - Sodium: 102mg

Ingredients:

- 1 tbsp. of olive oil

- ½ cup of chopped onion

- ½ cup of chopped celery stalk

- 2 minced garlic cloves

- 2 cups of sliced zucchini

- 5 cups of low- sodium chicken broth

- 1 cup of chopped unsalted cooked chicken

- Freshly ground black pepper, to taste

- 2 tbsp. of fresh lemon juice

- 2 tbsp. of chopped fresh cilantro

Directions:

1. In a large pan, heat oil on medium heat.

2. Add onion and celery and sauté for about 8-9 minutes.

3. Add garlic and sauté for about 1 minute.

4. Add zucchini and broth and bring to a boil on high heat.

5. Reduce the heat to medium-low and simmer for about 5-10 minutes.

6. Add cooked chicken and simmer for about 5 minutes.

7. Stir in black pepper and lemon juice and remove from heat.

8. Serve hot with the garnishing of cilantro.

HEARTY TURKEY SOUP (4 SERVINGS, SERVING: 1 BOWL)

Per Serving, Calories: 115- Fat: 5.5g - Carbs: 5.5g - Protein: 11.3g - Fiber: 1.6g - Potassium: 299mg - Sodium: 112mg

Ingredients:

- 2 tsp. of olive oil

- 6-ounce of lean ground turkey

- ½ cup of chopped scallion

- 2 minced garlic cloves

- 1 seeded and chopped Serrano pepper

- 2 cups of shredded cabbage

- ½ cup of chopped tomatoes

- 4 cups of low-sodium chicken broth

- Freshly ground black pepper, to taste

Directions:

1. In a large pan, heat oil on medium heat.

2. Add turkey and cook for about 6-7 minutes.

3. Add scallion and garlic and sauté for about 2-3 minutes.

4. Drain off excess fat from pan.

5. Add cabbage, tomatoes and broth and bring to a boil.

6. Reduce the heat to low and simmer, covered for about 15-20 minutes or till desired doneness.

7. Stir in black pepper and serve hot.

ENTICING VEGGIE SOUP (8 SERVINGS, SERVING: 1 BOWL)

Per Serving, Calories: 73- Fat: 3.7g - Carbs: 6.8g - Protein: 3.6g - Fiber: 2g - Potassium: 247mg - Sodium: 93mg

Ingredients:

- 2 tbsp. of olive oil

- 1 chopped large onion

- 2 chopped celery stalks

- ½ tsp. of red chili powder

- 1 cup of finely chopped tomatoes

- 3 cups of small cauliflower florets

- 3 cups of small broccoli florets

- 8 cups of low-sodium vegetable broth

- 2 tbsp. of fresh lemon juice

Directions:

1. In a large pan, heat oil on medium heat.

2. Add onion and celery and sauté for about 5-6 minutes.

3. Add chili powder and tomatoes and cook for about 2-3 minutes, crushing with the back of spoon.

4. Add cauliflower, broccoli and broth and bring to a boil on high heat.

5. Reduce the heat to low. Cover and simmer for about 30-35 minutes.

6. Stir in lemon juice and black pepper and remove from heat.

7. Serve hot.

SOUL WARMING STEW (10 SERVINGS, SERVING: 1 BOWL)

Per Serving, Calories: 150- Fat: 4.9g - Carbs: 4g - Protein: 21.5g - Fiber: 0g - Potassium: 276mg - Sodium: 144mg

Ingredients:

- 1 tbsp. of canola oil

- 1 finely chopped medium onion

- 1½ tsp. of minced garlic, divided

- ¼ tsp. of red pepper flakes, crushed

- 1 tsp. of finely grated fresh lemon peel

- ¼ pound of seeded and finely chopped plum tomatoes

- 2 cups of low-sodium chicken broth

- 1 pound of 1-inch cubed cod fillets

- 1 pound of peeled and deveined large shrimp

- 1/3 cup fresh parsley, chopped finely

- 1/3 cup of low-sodium mayonnaise

Directions:

1. In a large pan, heat oil on medium heat.

2. Add onion and sauté for about 4-6 minutes.

3. Add ½ tsp. of garlic and red pepper flakes and sauté for about 1 minute.

4. Add lemon peel and tomatoes and cook, stirring for about 2-3 minutes.

5. Add tomato paste and broth and bring to a boil.

6. Reduce the heat to low and simmer, covered for about 10 minutes.

7. Stir in seafood and parsley and simmer, covered for about 8-10 minutes or till desired doneness.

8. Remove from heat and transfer the stew in serving bowls.

9. In a small bowl, mix together remaining garlic and mayonnaise.

10. Top the stew with garlic mayo evenly and serve.

Mushroom Combo Stew (5 servings, serving: 1 bowl)

Per Serving, Calories: 110- Fat: 5,9g - Carbs: 13.6g - Protein: 3.2g - Fiber: 2.6g - Potassium: 289mg - Sodium: 129mg

Ingredients:

- 2 tbsp. of canola oil

- 2 chopped onions

- 3 minced garlic cloves

- ½ pound of chopped fresh button mushrooms

- ½ pound of chopped fresh shiitake mushrooms

- Freshly ground black pepper, to taste

- 1 cup of low-sodium vegetable broth

- 1 tbsp. of fresh lemon juice

- 2 chopped scallions

Directions:

1. In a large skillet, heat oil on medium heat.

2. Add onion and garlic and sauté for about 4-5 minutes.

3. Add mushrooms, salt and black pepper and cook for about 4-5 minutes.

4. Add broth and bring to a gentle boil.

5. Simmer for about 4-5 minutes or till desired doneness.

6. Stir in lemon juice and scallion and remove from heat.

7. Serve hot.

Fiesta Chicken Thighs (4 servings, serving: 1 chicken thigh)

Per Serving, Calories: 150- Fat: 4.3g - Carbs: 1.6g - Protein: 25.6g - Fiber: 0.6g - Potassium: 36mg - Sodium: 81mg

Ingredients:

- 2 minced garlic cloves

- ½ tbsp. of minced fresh thyme

- ½ tbsp. of minced fresh rosemary

- ½ tsp. of ground cumin

- ½ tbsp. of crushed red pepper flakes

- Pinch of salt

- Freshly ground black pepper, to taste

- 1 tbsp. of fresh lemon juice

- 4 (4-ounce) skinless, boneless chicken thighs

Directions:

1. Preheat the grill to medium-high heat. Grease the grill grate.

2. For chicken in a bowl, add all ingredients except chicken thighs and mix till well combined.

3. Coat the thighs with spice mixture generously.

4. Grill the chicken thighs for about 8 minutes per side.

DISTINCTIVE CHICKEN BREASTS (4 SERVINGS, SERVING: 1 CHICKEN BREAST HALF)

Per Serving, Calories: 200- Fat: 10.1g - Carbs: 0.4g - Protein: 26g - Fiber: 0g - Potassium: 11mg - Sodium: 123mg

Ingredients:

- 4 (4-ounce) skinless, boneless chicken breast halves

- 2 tbsp. of melted unsalted margarine

- 1 tbsp. of low-fat Parmesan cheese

- 1 minced garlic clove

- ¼ cup of minced fresh basil

- Freshly ground black pepper, to taste

Directions:

1. Preheat the oven to 325 degrees F.

2. With a fork, pierce each chicken breast at several places and arrange into a glass baking dish in a single layer.

3. In a bowl mix together remaining ingredients,

4. Place the margarine mixture over chicken breasts evenly.

5. Bake for about 25 minutes, basting with the pan mixture after every 10 minutes.

SUCCULENT CHICKEN & GREEN BEANS (4 SERVINGS, SERVING: 1 PORTION)

Per Serving, Calories: 171- Fat: 7.1g - Carbs: 6.3g - Protein: 21.4g - Fiber: 3g - Potassium: 169mg - Sodium: 71mg

Ingredients:

- 1 tbsp. of olive oil

- 2 (6-ounce) skinless, boneless chicken breasts

- 2 tbsp. of curry powder

- 2 cups of low-sodium chicken broth

- 2 cups of trimmed and cut into 1-inch size fresh green beans

- Freshly ground black pepper, to taste

- ¼ cup fresh cilantro leaves, chopped

Directions:

1. In a skillet, heat oil on medium heat.

2. Add chicken and cook for about 8-10 minutes.

3. Add curry powder and cook for about 1 minute.

4. Add broth and bring to a boil.

5. Reduce the heat low and simmer for about 8-10 minutes.

6. With a slotted spoon, transfer the chicken onto a plate.

7. With a sharp knife, cut chicken into small pieces.

8. Add chicken, green beans and black pepper and cook for about 4-5 minutes or till desired doneness.

9. Serve with the garnishing of cilantro.

PARTIES SPECIAL MEAL (6 SERVINGS, SERVING: 1 PORTION)

Per Serving, Calories: 128- Fat: 4g - Carbs: 14.9g - Protein: 9.8g - Fiber: 2.3g - Potassium: 243mg - Sodium: 18mg

Ingredients:

- 1 tbsp. of olive oil

- 1 chopped large onion

- 1 minced garlic clove

- 1 tsp. of minced fresh ginger

- 2 cubed skinless, boneless chicken breasts

- 2 cups of cube fresh pineapple

- 1 seeded and chopped tomato

- 1 seeded and chopped medium red bell pepper

- 1 seeded and chopped medium green bell pepper

- 1 seeded and chopped medium orange bell pepper

- 2 tbsp. of apple cider vinegar

- Freshly ground black pepper, to taste

Directions:

1. In a large skillet, heat oil on medium heat.

2. Add onion and sauté for about 4-5 minutes.

3. Add garlic and ginger and sauté for about 1 minute.

4. Add chicken and cook for about 10 minutes or till browned from all sides.

5. Add pineapple, tomatoes and bell peppers and cook for about 5-7 minutes or till vegetables become tender.

6. Add vinegar and pepper and cook for about 2-3 minutes.

7. Serve hot.

RICHLY FLAVORED CHICKEN (6 SERVINGS, SERVING: 1 PORTION)

Per Serving, Calories: 199- Fat: 8.3g - Carbs: 3.4g - Protein: 25.8g - Fiber: 0.8g - Potassium: 45mg - Sodium: 70mg

Ingredients:

- 1 tbsp. of olive oil

- 6 (4-ounce) skinless, boneless chicken thighs

- ¼ cup of finely chopped onion

- 1¼ cups of low-sodium chicken broth

- 1 cup of fresh cranberries

- ½ tbsp. of sugar

- 1 tbsp. of unsalted butter

- Freshly ground black pepper, to taste

- 2 tbsp. of fresh lemon juice

Directions:

1. In a large skillet, heat oil on medium heat.

2. Add the chicken and cook for about 5-7 minutes per side.

3. Transfer the chicken into a large bowl.

4. Cover with a piece of foil to keep the chicken warm.

5. In the same skillet, add onion on medium heat and sauté for about 2-3 minutes.

6. Add broth and bring to a boil, stirring occasionally to loosen the brown bits from the bottom.

7. Stir in cranberries and cook or about 5 minutes.

8. Stir in sugar and black pepper and cook for about 1-2 minutes.

9. Stir in butter and remove from heat.

10. Pour cranberry mixture over chicken and serve.

CROWD-PLEASING CHICKEN (8 SERVINGS, SERVING: ½ BREAST ROLL)

Per Serving, Calories: 145- Fat: 6.7g - Carbs: 0.5g - Protein: 20.2g - Fiber: 0g - Potassium: 12mg - Sodium: 83mg

Ingredients:

For Stuffing:

- 2 minced garlic cloves

- 3 tbsp. of chopped fresh basil

- ¼ cup of grated Parmesan cheese

- 1 tbsp. of melted unsalted butter

- 4 (6-ounce) pounded to 1/8-inch thickness skinless, boneless chicken breast halves

For Sauce:

- 1 tbsp. of melted unsalted butter

- 2 tbsp. of fresh lemon juice

- ½ tsp. of finely grated fresh lemon zest

Directions:

1. Preheat the outdoor grill to medium heat. Grease the grill grate.

2. For stuffing in a small bowl, mix together all ingredients except breast halves.

3. Arrange breast halves onto smooth surface. Place cheese stuffing over the center of each breast half.

4. Fold the sides and then roll up each breast half. With toothpicks, secure the breast rolls.

5. Grill for about 10 minutes.

6. Meanwhile for sauce in another small bowl, mix together all ingredients.

7. Coat the rolls with sauce evenly and grill for 10 minutes more.

8. Remove from the grill and cut each roll in 2 equal sized portions.

IRRESISTIBLE CREAMY CHICKEN (4 SERVINGS, SERVING: 1 PORTION)

Per Serving, Calories: 206- Fat: 10.5g - Carbs: 1.2g - Protein: 26.1g - Fiber: 0g - Potassium: 43mg - Sodium: 144mg

Ingredients:

- 3 tbsp. of unsalted butter

- 2 pound of cut into 1-inch thick strips skinless, boneless chicken breasts

- 4 minced garlic cloves

- ½ tsp. of ground ginger

- ½ tsp. of ground coriander

- ½ tsp. of ground cumin

- ¼ tsp. of crushed red pepper flakes

- ½ cup of chicken broth

- 1/3 cup of low-fat sour cream

- 1 tbsp. of chopped fresh parsley

Directions:

1. In a large skillet, melt butter on medium-high heat.

2. Add chicken and cook for about 5-6 minutes.

3. Add garlic and spices and cook for 1 minute.

4. Add broth and bring to a boil. Reduce the heat to medium-low.

5. Simmer for about 5 minutes, stirring occasionally.

6. Stir in cream and simmer, stirring occasionally for about 3 minutes.

7. Serve hot with the garnishing of parsley.

FABULOUS CHICKEN (8 SERVINGS, SERVING: 1 PORTION)

Per Serving, Calories: 279 - Fat: 11.2g - Carbs: 18.8g - Protein: 26.4g - Fiber: 3.8g – Potassium: 145mg – Sodium: 60mg

Ingredients:

- 1 cup of low-sodium chicken broth

- 3 tbsp. of balsamic vinegar

- 2 tsp. of cornstarch

- 2 tbsp. of olive oil

- 4 minced garlic cloves

- 2 tbsp. of minced fresh basil

- 4 (4-ounce) skinless, boneless chicken breasts

- Pinch of salt

- Freshly ground black pepper, to taste

- 2 cored and sliced pears

Directions:

1. In a bowl, mix together broth, vinegar and cornstarch.

2. In a large skillet, heat oil on medium-high heat.

3. Add garlic and basil and sauté for about 1 minute.

4. Add chicken and sprinkle with salt and black pepper.

5. Cook for about 12-15 minutes. Transfer the chicken into a bowl.

6. In the same skillet, add pears and cook for about 4-5 minutes.

7. Add broth mixture and bring to a boil, cook for about 1 minute.

8. Reduce the heat to low.

9. Stir in chicken and cook for about 3-4 minutes.

DIVINE GROUND CHICKEN (5 SERVINGS, SERVING: 1 PORTION)

Per Serving, Calories: 164- Fat: 6.2g - Carbs: 2.9g - Protein: 23.5g - Fiber: 0.7g - Potassium: 161mg - Sodium: 99mg

Ingredients:

- 1¼ pound of lean ground chicken

- 1 sliced small onion

- 2 tsp. of minced garlic

- 1 tsp. of ground cumin

- 1 tsp. of ground coriander

- 1/8 tsp. of ground turmeric

- 1/8 tsp. of cayenne pepper

- Pinch of salt

- Freshly ground black pepper

- 1 chopped medium tomato

- 1 cup of water

- ¼ cup of chopped fresh cilantro, chopped

Directions:

1. Heat a nonstick skillet on medium-high heat.

2. Add chicken, onion and garlic and cook for about 5-6 minutes or till browned.

3. Remove any excess fat from skillet.

4. Add spices and tomato cook for about 2 minutes.

5. Stir in water and bring to a gentle boil.

6. Reduce the heat to medium-low an, simmer, covered for about 10-15 minutes.

7. Stir in cilantro and serve immediately.

COMFORTING CHICKEN CHILI (12 SERVINGS, SERVING: 1 POTION)

Per Serving, Calories: 155- Fat: 6.7g - Carbs: 7.4g - Protein: 17.1g - Fiber: 1.6g - Potassium: 275mg - Sodium: 123mg

Ingredients:

- 2 tbsp. of olive oil

- 1 chopped large onion

- 1 seeded and chopped medium green bell pepper

- 1 seeded and chopped medium red bell pepper

- 4 minced garlic cloves

- 1 chopped jalapeño pepper

- 1 tsp. of crushed dried basil

- 1 tsp. of crushed dried thyme

- 1 tbsp. of red chili powder

- 1 tbsp. of ground cumin

- 2 pound of lean ground chicken

- 8-ounce of low-sodium tomato paste

- 2 cups of low-sodium chicken broth

- 2 cups of water

Directions:

1. In a large pan, heat oil on medium heat.

2. Add onion and bell pepper and sauté for about 5-7 minutes.

3. Add garlic, jalapeño pepper, herbs, spices and black pepper and sauté for about 1 minute.

4. Add chicken and cook for about 4-5 minutes.

5. Stir in tomato paste and cook for about 2 minutes.

6. Add broth and water and bring to a boil.

7. Reduce the heat to low and simmer, covered for about 1-1½ hours or till desired doneness.

8. Serve hot.

QUICK-AND-EASY STEAK (8 SERVINGS, SERVING: ½ STEAK)

Per Serving, Calories: 279- Fat: 19.5g - Carbs: 0g - Protein: 22.4g - Fiber: 0g - Potassium: 1mg - Sodium: 56mg

Ingredients:

- 4 (½-pound) trimmed beef top sirloin steaks

- 2 tbsp. of olive oil

- 2 tsp. of Mrs. Dash salt-free herb seasoning

Directions:

1. Preheat the grill for high heat. Grease the grill grate.

2. Drizzle the steaks with oil and ten rub with seasoning evenly.

3. Grill the steaks for about 4-5 minutes per side or till desired doneness.

4. Cut each steak in half and serve.

EXCEPTIONAL STEAK (16 SERVINGS, SERVING: 1 POTION)

Per Serving, Calories: 166 - Fat: 7.2g - Carbs: 0.2g - Protein: 23.7g - Fiber: 0g - Potassium: 295mg -Sodium: 70mg

Ingredients:

- ¼ tsp. of ground cumin

- 1 tsp. of red chili powder

- Pinch of salt

- Freshly ground black pepper, to taste

- 1¼-pound of trimmed flank steak

Directions:

1. Preheat the grill to medium heat. Grease the grill grate.

2. In a large bowl, mix together all ingredients except steak.

3. Add steak and coat with spice mixture generously.

4. Place the steak on grill over medium coals.

5. Grill for about 17-21 minutes, flipping once in the middle way.

6. Remove the steak from grill and keep aside for about 5-10 minutes before slicing.

7. With a sharp knife, cut the steak into desired size slices.

CONTEST-WINNING MEATLOAF (10 SERVINGS, SERVING: 1 PORTION)

Per Serving, Calories: 150- Fat: 4.5g - Carbs: 4.7g - Protein: 21.4g - Fiber: 0.8g - Potassium: 300mg - Sodium: 133mg

Ingredients:

- 1½ pound of lean ground beef

- ¼ cup of rolled oats

- ½ cup of shredded zucchini

- ¼ cup of finely chopped onion

- 1 tsp. of minced garlic, divided

- 3 tbsp. of chopped fresh parsley, divided

- 1 tsp. of crushed dried thyme

- Freshly ground black pepper, to taste

- 8-ounce low-sodium pizza sauce, divided

Directions:

1. Grease a 9-inch microwave safe pie plate. Keep aside.

2. In a large bowl, add turkey, beef, oats, zucchini, onion, ½ tsp. of garlic, 2 tbsp. of parsley, thyme, salt, black pepper and 2 tbsp. of pizza sauce and mix till well combined.

3. Make a 7x4x2-inch sized loaf from mixture.

4. Arrange meatloaf onto prepared pie plate.

5. With a large parchment paper, cover the pie plate.

6. Microwave on high for about 5 minutes, turning once in the middle way.

7. Remove from microwave and remove the drippings.

8. In a bowl, mix together remaining garlic, parsley and pizza sauce.

9. Spread sauce mixture over meatloaf evenly.

10. Cover with parchment paper and microwave on 50% power for about 21-24 minutes, rotating plate twice.

APPEALING STEAK (2 SERVINGS, SERVING: 1 STEAK)

Per Serving, Calories: 122- Fat: 5.4g - Carbs: 0.2g - Protein: 16.3g - Fiber: 1.8g – Potassium: 11mg – Sodium: 42mg

Ingredients:

- 2 (4-ounce) fillet mignon steaks

- Pinch of salt

- Freshly ground black pepper, to taste

- ¼ cup of low-sodium chicken broth

- ¼ cup of balsamic vinegar

Directions:

1. Heat a large nonstick skillet on medium-high heat.

2. Add steaks and sprinkle with salt and black pepper.

3. Cook for about 1 minute per side.

4. Stir in broth and vinegar and immediately, reduce the heat to medium-low.

5. Cover and cook for about 4 minutes. Uncover and flip the side.

6. Coat the steaks with glaze and cook, covered for about 4 minutes more.

7. Serve the steaks with the topping of glaze from pan.

FLAVORFUL PORK CHOPS (4 SERVINGS, SERVING: 1 CHOP)

Per Serving, Calories: 267- Fat: 13.5g - Carbs: 0.9g - Protein: 35.9g - Fiber: 0g - Potassium: 20mg - Sodium: 41mg

Ingredients:

- ¼ cup of minced fresh basil

- 2 minced garlic cloves

- 2 tbsp. of olive oil

- 2 tbsp. of fresh lemon juice

- Pinch of salt

- Freshly ground black pepper, to taste

- 4 bone-in pork loin chops

Directions:

1. In a large bowl, mix together all ingredients except chops.

2. Add chops and coat with mixture generously.

3. Cover and keep aside to marinate for about 30-45 minutes.

4. Preheat the grill to medium-high heat. Grease the grill grate.

5. Grill for about 6 minutes per side.

IMPRESSIVE COD CASSEROLE (5 SERVINGS, SERVING: 1 PORTION)

Per Serving, Calories: 143- Fat: 5.4g - Carbs: 1.3g - Protein: 21.5g - Fiber: 0.6g - Potassium: 299mg - Sodium: 125mg

Ingredients:

- 2 tbsp. of unsalted margarine

- ¼ cup of chopped onion

- 1½ cups of sliced fresh mushrooms

- 1 pound of fresh cod fillets

- Freshly ground black pepper, to taste

- 1 tsp. of crushed dried thyme

Directions:

1. Preheat the oven to 450 degrees F.

2. In a skillet, melt margarine on medium heat.

3. Add onion and mushrooms and sauté for about 5-6 minutes.

4. Arrange the cod fillets in a baking dish and top with mushroom mixture evenly.

5. Sprinkle with black pepper and thyme

6. Bake for about 12-15 minutes.

OMEGA-3 RICH SALMON (2 SERVINGS, SERVING: 1 FILLET)

Per Serving, Calories: 265- Fat: 19.2g - Carbs: 0.5g - Protein: 22.3g - Fiber: 0g - Potassium: 23mg - Sodium: 146mg

Ingredients:

- 2 (4-ounce) skinless, boneless salmon fillets

- 2 tbsp. of fresh lemon juice

- 1 tbsp. of olive oil

- ¼ tsp. of crushed dried oregano

- Pinch of salt

- Freshly ground black pepper, to taste

Directions:

1. Preheat the oven to 425 degrees F. Line a baking sheet with parchment paper.

2. Place the salmon fillets onto prepared baking sheet.

3. Drizzle with lemon juice and oil evenly and sprinkle with oregano, salt and black pepper.

4. Bake for about 20-25 minutes.

5. Serve hot.

Wholesome Salmon Meal (6 servings, serving: 1 portion)

Per Serving, Calories: 233- Fat: 14.5g - Carbs: 2.5g - Protein: 22.9g - Fiber: 0.8g - Potassium: 173mg - Sodium: 71mg

Ingredients:

- 4 (6-ounce) (1-inch thick) skinless salmon fillets

- Freshly ground black pepper, to taste

- 2 cups of finely chopped zucchini, chopped finely

- 1 cup of halved cherry tomatoes

- 1 tbsp. of olive oil

- 1 tbsp. of fresh lemon juice

Directions:

1. Preheat the oven to 425 degrees F. Grease an 11x7-inch baking dish.

2. Place the salmon fillets in prepared baking dish in a single layer and sprinkle with black pepper generously.

3. In a bowl, mix together remaining ingredients.

4. Place the mixture over salmon fillets evenly.

5. Bake for about 22 minutes.

6. Remove from the oven and keep aside to cool slightly.

7. Cut the salmon into small chunks and mix with veggie mixture.

8. Serve warm.

SUCCULENT TILAPIA (4 SERVINGS, SERVING: 1 FILLET)

Per Serving, Calories: 149- Fat: 6.7g - Carbs: 1.1g - Protein: 21.4g - Fiber: 0g - Potassium: 17mg - Sodium: 107mg

Ingredients:

- 2 tbsp. of unsalted margarine

- 4 minced garlic cloves

- 1 tsp. of chopped fresh parsley

- Freshly ground black pepper, to taste

- Pinch of Mrs. Dash salt-free herb seasoning

- 4 (4-ounce) tilapia fillets

Directions:

1. Preheat the oven to 350 degrees F. Line a shallow baking dish with a piece of foil.

2. In a large nonstick skillet, add margarine, garlic, parsley, black pepper and seasoning on low heat.

3. Cook till melted completely, stirring continuously.

4. Remove from heat.

5. In the bottom of a prepared baking dish, spread a little of the garlic sauce evenly.

6. Arrange the tilapia fillets over the garlic sauce.

7. Coat the top of each tilapia fillet with the garlic sauce evenly.

8. Bake for about 12-15 minutes.

FESTIVE TILAPIA (8 SERVINGS, SERVING: 1 FILLET)

Per Serving, Calories: 176- Fat: 9.1g - Carbs: 1.2g - Protein: 22.9g - Fiber: 0g -
Potassium: 7mg - Sodium: 156mg

Ingredients:

- 1/3 cup of shredded low-fat Parmesan cheese

- 2 tbsp. of low-sodium mayonnaise

- ¼ cup of softened unsalted butter

- 2 tbsp. of fresh lemon juice

- 2 pound of tilapia fillets

- ¼ tsp. of crushed dried thyme

- Freshly ground black pepper, to taste

Directions:

a. Preheat the broiler. Grease the broiler pan.

b. In a large bowl, mix together all ingredients except tilapia fillets. Keep aside.

c. Place the fillets onto prepared broiler pan in a single layer.

d. Broil the fillets for about 2-3 minutes.

e. Remove from oven and top the fillets with cheese mixture evenly.

f.   Broil for about 2 minutes more.

FAMILY GET-TOGETHER CASSEROLE (8 SERVINGS, SERVING: 1 PORTION)

Per Serving, Calories: 161- Fat: 6.6g - Carbs: 4.2g - Protein: 18.8g - Fiber: 0.6g - Potassium: 249mg - Sodium: 290mg

Ingredients:

- 2 tbsp. of olive oil

- 1 tbsp. of minced garlic

- 1½ pound of peeled and deveined large shrimp

- ¾ tsp. of crushed dried oregano

- ¼ tsp. of crushed red pepper flakes

- ¼ cup of chopped fresh parsley

- 1 cup of low-sodium chicken broth

- 2 tbsp. of fresh lemon juice

- 1½ cups of finely chopped tomatoes

- 4-ounce of crumbled feta cheese

Directions:

1. Preheat the oven to 350 degrees F.

2. In a large skillet, melt butter on medium-high heat.

3. Add garlic and sauté for about 1 minute.

4. Add shrimp, oregano and red pepper flakes and cook for about 3-4 minutes.

5. Stir in parsley and salt and immediately transfer into a casserole dish evenly.

6. In the same skillet, add broth and lemon juice on medium heat and boil for about 4-5 minutes.

7. Stir in tomatoes and cook for about 2-3 minutes.

8. Pour the tomato mixture over shrimp mixture evenly.

9. Top with cheese evenly.

10. Bake for about 15-20 minutes or till top becomes golden brown.

FAMILY HIT CURRY (8 SERVINGS, SERVING: 1 BOWL)

Per Serving, Calories: 191 - Fat: 5.3g - Carbs: 5g - Protein: 29.2g - Fiber: 0g - Potassium: 270mg - Sodium: 199mg

Ingredients:

- 1½ tbsp. of canola oil

- 1 finely chopped onion

- 1 tsp. of minced fresh ginger

- 3 minced garlic cloves

- 1 tbsp. of curry paste

- 2 cups of fat-free plain Greek yogurt

- ¼ cup of water

- 1 tsp. of sugar

- 1 pound of cubed cod fillets

- 1 pound of peeled and deveined prawns

- Pinch of salt

- Freshly ground black pepper, to taste

- 2 tbsp. of fresh lemon juice

- ¼ cup of chopped fresh cilantro leaves

Directions:

1. In a large pan, heat oil on medium heat. Add onion and sauté for about 4-5 minutes.

2. Add ginger, garlic and curry paste and sauté for about 1 minute.

3. Stir in yogurt, water and sugar and bring to a boil on high heat.

4. Reduce the heat to medium-low. Simmer for about 5 minutes.

5. Stir in seafood and cook for about 10 minutes or till desired thickness.

6. Stir in salt, black pepper, lemon juice and cilantro and remove from heat.

7. Serve hot.

FLAVORSOME VEGGIES CURRY (6 SERVINGS, SERVING: 1 BOWL)

Per Serving, Calories: 83- Fat: 5g - Carbs: 9.6g - Protein: 1.6g - Fiber: 1g - Potassium: 294mg - Sodium: 12mg

Ingredients:

- 1 chopped medium zucchini

- 1 chopped medium yellow squash

- 1 sccdcd and cubed green bell peppers

- 1 seeded and cubed red bell pepper

- 1 thinly sliced onion

- 1 tbsp. of maple syrup

- 2 tbsp. of canola oil

- 2 tsp. of curry powder

- Freshly ground black pepper, to taste

- ¼ cup of low-sodium vegetable broth

- ¼ cup of chopped fresh cilantro

Directions:

1. Preheat the oven to 375 degrees F. Lightly, grease a large baking dish.

2. In a large bowl, add all ingredients except cilantro and mix well.

3. Transfer the vegetables mixture into prepared baking dish.

4. Bake for about 15-20 minutes.

5. Serve immediately with the garnishing of cilantro.

Richly Tasty Mushroom Curry (6 servings, serving: 1 bowl)

Per Serving, Calories: 98- Fat: 5.1g - Carbs: 13.1g - Protein: 2.2g - Fiber: 2.2g - Potassium: 263mg - Sodium: 113mg

Ingredients:

- 1¼ cups of chopped tomatoes

- 1 chopped green chili

- 1 tsp. of chopped fresh ginger

- 2 tbsp. of canola oil

- ½ tsp. of ground cumin

- ¼ tsp. of ground coriander

- ¼ tsp. of ground turmeric

- ¼ tsp. of red chili powder

- 1½ cups of sliced fresh shiitake mushrooms

- 1½ cups of sliced fresh button mushrooms

- 1 cup of frozen corn kernels

- 1½ cups of water

Directions:

1. In a food processor, add tomatoes, green chili and ginger and pulse till a smooth paste forms.

2. In a pan, heat oil on medium heat.

3. Add spices and sauté for about 1 minute.

4. Add tomato paste and cook for about 4-5 minutes.

5. Stir in mushrooms, corn and water and cook, stirring occasionally for about 10-12 minutes.

6. Serve warm.

CLASSIC BARLEY WITH MUSHROOMS (6 SERVINGS, SERVING: 1 PORTION)

Per Serving, Calories: 153- Fat: 2.8g - Carbs: 27.9g - Protein: 4.8g - Fiber: 5.6g - Potassium: 149mg - Sodium: 39mg

Ingredients:

- 1 tbsp. of canola oil

- 1 chopped small onion, chopped

- 1 cup of sliced fresh mushrooms

- 3 cups of low-sodium vegetable broth

- 1 cup of pearl barley

- Pinch of freshly ground black pepper

- 2 tbsp. of chopped fresh cilantro leaves

Directions:

1. In a large pan, heat oil on medium heat.

2. Add onion and mushrooms and sauté for about 4 to 5 minutes.

3. Add soup, barley and black pepper and bring to a boil.

4. Reduce the heat to low and simmer, covered for about 45 minutes or till all liquid is absorbed.

5. Transfer the barley mixture into serving plates.

6. Garnish with cilantro and serve.

SCRUMPTIOUS BARLEY RISOTTO (6 SERVINGS, SERVING: 1 PLATE)

Per Serving, Calories: 115- Fat: 4.8g - Carbs: 16.7g - Protein: 2.1g - Fiber: 3.7g - Potassium: 131mg - Sodium: 5mg

Ingredients:

- 1 cup of water

- ½ cup of pearl barley

- 2 tbsp. of vegetable oil, divided

- 2 minced garlic cloves

- 1 seeded and chopped small jalapeño pepper

- ½ cup of chopped onion

- ½ cup of seeded and chopped red bell pepper

- 1 cup of thinly sliced eggplant

- 2 tbsp. of chopped fresh mint leaves

- 2 tbsp. of chopped fresh cilantro

- 1/8 tsp. of crushed red pepper flakes

- 1 tsp. of sugar

Directions:

1. In a pan, add water and barley on medium-high heat and bring to a boil.

2. Immediately, reduce the heat to low and simmer, covered for about 45 minutes or till all the liquid is absorbed.

3. In a large skillet, heat 1 tbsp. of oil on high heat.

4. Add garlic and jalapeño pepper and sauté for about 1 minute.

5. Stir in cooked barley and cook for about 3 minutes.

6. Remove from heat and keep aside.

7. In another skillet, heat remaining oil on medium on medium heat.

8. Add onion and sauté for about 4-5 minutes.

9. Add bell pepper and eggplant and stir fry for about 3 minutes.

10. Stir in remaining ingredients and cook for about 2-3 minutes.

11. Stir in barley mixture and cook for about 2-3 minutes.

12. Serve hot.

SUPERB CRANBERRY PILAF (4 SERVINGS, SERVING: 1 PLATE)

Per Serving, Calories: 213- Fat: 6.4g - Carbs: 33.3g - Protein: 4.4g - Fiber: 2.1g - Potassium: 99mg - Sodium: 96mg

Ingredients:

- 2 tbsp. of unsalted butter

- 1 cup of chopped onion

- 2 tsp. of minced garlic

- ¾ cup of Arborio rice

- ½ cup of dried cranberries

- 2 cups of low-sodium vegetable broth

- 1 tbsp. of low-fat Parmesan cheese

Directions:

1. Preheat the oven to 425 degrees F. Grease a casserole dish.

2. In a large pan, melt the butter on medium heat.

3. Add onion and garlic and sauté for about 5 minutes.

4. Add rice and sauté for about 2 minutes.

5. Add cranberries and broth and bring to a boil.

6. Cook for about 2 minutes.

7. Transfer the rice mixture into the prepared casserole dish evenly.

8. Cover the casserole dish and bake for about 30 minutes.

9. Remove from oven and immediately, sprinkle with cheese evenly.

10. Serve immediately.

GOURMET DINNER MEAL (7 SERVINGS, SERVING: 1 PORTION)

Per Serving, Calories: 216- Fat: 11.4g - Carbs: 24.4g - Protein: 5g - Fiber: 1.5g
- Potassium: 300mg - Sodium: 15mg

Ingredients:

- 1 cup of grape tomatoes

- 1/3 cup of vegetable oil, divided

- Freshly ground black pepper, to taste

- 1 seeded and chopped small red bell pepper

- 1 seeded and chopped small red bell pepper

- 1 chopped small yellow squash

- 1 chopped small zucchini

- 1 chopped medium onion

- 6 minced garlic cloves

- 2 tbsp. of balsamic vinegar

- ½ tsp. of crushed red pepper flakes

- ¼ tsp. of ground cumin

- 8-ounce of spaghetti

- ¼ cup of chopped fresh basil

Directions:

1. Preheat the oven to 425 degrees F. Arrange 2 racks in the middle position of oven.

2. In a roasting pan, add tomatoes, 2 tbsp. of oil and a pinch of black pepper. Keep aside.

3. In a large bowl, add vegetables, onion, garlic, vinegar, spices, black pepper and remaining oil and toss to coat well.

4. Transfer the vegetable mixture into another roasting pan in a single layer.

5. Arrange the rack tomatoes on the lower rack of oven.

6. Arrange the rack of vegetables on the upper rack of oven.

7. Roast for about 20 minutes.

8. Remove the roasting pans from oven.

9. Flip the vegetables and roast for about 10 minutes.

10. Meanwhile in a pan of salted boiling water, add pasta and cook for about 8-10 minutes or according to package's directions.

11. Drain well, reserving 1 cup of cooking liquid.

12. Transfer the pasta into a large bowl.

13. Add the cherry tomatoes with all the pan juices and a splash of reserved cooking liquid and toss to coat well.

14. Add roasted vegetables and toss to coat well.

15. Serve hot with the garnishing of basil.

CHAPTER 4: CONCLUSION

Thank you again for picking up this cookbook! I hope it was able to help you to find a wide variety of healthy, and delicious sounding recipes that you can't wait to try for yourself.

Finally, if you enjoyed this book, then I'd like to ask you for a favor, would you be kind enough to leave a review for this book on Amazon? It'd be greatly appreciated!

Made in the USA
Lexington, KY
27 June 2018